THE RESEARCH ON ANTICANCER
TRADITIONAL CHINESE MEDICATION

with

IMMUNE REGULATION AND CONTROL

Volume IV

——Experimental research and clinical
application verification

Authors: Xu Ze (China) ; Xu Jie(China) ; Bin Wu(America)
Translators: Bin Wu ; Lily Xu ; Zihao Xu ; Bo Wu
Editors: Bin Wu, Lily Xu, Tao Wu
Illustrators: Lily Xu, Bin Wu

authorHOUSE®

AuthorHouse™
1663 Liberty Drive
Bloomington, IN 47403
www.authorhouse.com
Phone: 1 (800) 839-8640

Published by AuthorHouse 02/25/2019

ISBN: 978-1-7283-0037-5 (sc)
ISBN: 978-1-7283-0036-8 (e)

Library of Congress Control Number: 2019901703

Print information available on the last page.

Contents

Introduction to this book

Bin Wu

Science is endless and the road on science or our research life is not always smooth and **only those who are not afraid of failure, or hard work, or difficulties can reach the summit of the life or science mountain**. The surgeon and professor **Dr. Xu Ze** in China is an example for us to learn on searching the oncology treatment and the new medications, who put hours and hours time in the operating rooms and in the animal rooms to search for the answer: <u>understanding what Cancer is</u> ? how can cancer be treated and be cured? How to help the cancer patients to live longer and to get the treatment and to get rid of all of the fear? how can we improve cancer care? How can cancer be prevented? Challenging scientific thinking and **unbeatable surgical skills** and **unlimited dedication** to the patients lead to all of these innovation discoveries on cancer medications and the new concepts of cancer and the new methods on the cancer treatment. Excellent surgery skills were very important to finish all of these difficult experiments. An excellent surgeon should be like an excellent human tailor who can make a healthy and beautiful human body. A lot of experiments and a lot of failure and tons of hours were put inside. In summary, it is the dedication to the human being health and devotion to oncology medicine and all of other medicine.

Whenever each of these series of book is done and is published, my tear cannot help full of both of my eyes because each of word plumps our hard work and hours and day and night. In this volume it is described that all of detail experimental and clinical verification of how Dr. Xu Ze get all of these new treatments and new medications. This volume is mainly discussing pharmacology and immune pharmacology about Xu Ze's new discovery and new medications by immune control and regulation. Each word in this book comes from our hard work. In our practice the questions are found, then we come back to do the experiments to solve all of these questions; then come back to apply to our clinical practice to improve our patient care.

Finally, due to finishing the books in such a short time and there are huge information in the book and day and night hard work, if there is any mistake, please forgive us and look forward to the feedback.

Thanks again
Bin Wu, MD., Ph.D in Timonium in Maryland in USA
01-28-2019

This book's main topics

A. **The research on anticancer traditional Chinese medication with immune regulation and control**

——*Experimental research and clinical application verification*

- *Experimental research + clinical application + typical case + case list*
- *XZ-C immunomodulation anti-cancer Chinese medications are 48 kinds of Chinese herbal medicines with good tumor inhibition rate which were screened by anti-tumor experiments in cancer-bearing mice from the more than 200 traditional Chinese medicines in China. After the compound is compounded, then the tumor-inhibiting experiment is carried out in the cancer-bearing mice. The compound inhibition rate is greater than the single-taste inhibition rate, and XZ-C1 has a significant anti-tumor effect, and does not kill normal cells. For mouse sarcoma S_{180}, the tumor inhibition rate is as high as 98.9%, which has the effect of strengthening the body and supporting the rightness and improving the immune function of the human body.*

B. **The research on anticancer traditional Chinese medication with immune regulation and control**

——*Experimental research and clinical application verification*

- *Self-developed a series of XZ-C (XU ZE-China) (Xu Ze - China) anti-cancer traditional Chinese medicine preparations with immune regulation and control, which are from experimental research to clinical validation, applied to clinical practice based on the success of animal experiments. After more than 12,000 clinical trials in 34 years, the curative effect is remarkable, and it is independent innovation and independent intellectual property rights.*
- *A series products of exclusive research and development products XZ-C immune regulation and control anti-cancer Chinese medication (introduction)*
- *The range and scope of the clinical application of XZ-C$_{1-10}$ immunoregulation traditional Chinese medication for anti-cancer, metastasis, recurrence*
- *Typical cases*
- *List of cases*

C. **The research on anticancer traditional Chinese medication with immune regulation and control**

——*Experimental research and clinical application verification*

- *XZ-C pharmacodynamic study in our laboratory proves that it has a high tumor inhibition rate for Ehrlich ascites carcinoma, S_{180} and H_{22} hepatocellular carcinoma.*
- *There is no acute toxic side effects in the mouse acute toxicity tests. For the long-term oral administration in the clinic (after 2-6-8-10 years), there is no obvious side effects*
- *In general, in the advanced cancer patients, there are mostly weak and weak and tired and tired and loss of appetite. **After taking** XZ-C immunomodulatory Chinese medicine for 4-8-12-16 weeks, it can significantly improve appetite, sleep, relieve pain, gradually restore physical strength, and more likely to prolong survival.*

The research on XZ-C anticancer traditional Chinese medication with immune regulation and control

How to conquer cancer? How to prevent cancer? How to treat cancer? How to conquer cancer and to launch the general attack of cancer?

Professor Xu Ze (XZ-C) summed up the collection, agglutinated wisdom, and proposed 1 to 8 of "walked out of the new path to conquer cancer" in order to help or to facilitate clinical application and to become the clinical reference.

In the past 60 years, the series of the scientific research achievements and the series of scientific and technological innovations which **takes "conquer cancer" as the direction** done by us are in this series of "Monographs"; the following thesis or lemma are first proposed internationally, all of which are original papers, internationally pioneered, and have reached the forefront of the world.

XZ-C's scientific thinking, scientific research design, academic thinking, and scientific dedication about conquering cancer and launching the total cancer attack are summarized as the following monographs:

1. "Walked out of the new road to conquer cancer" (1)(一)
   "Conquer cancer and launch the total attack to cancer – the prevention of cancer and cancer control and cancer treatment at the same level and at the same time and at the same attention"

2. "Walked out of a new road to conquer cancer" (2) (二)
   "Walked out of a new way of cancer treatment with immune control and regulation of the combination of Chinese and Western medicine"
   (Part I), (Part 2)

3. "Walk out of the new road to conquer cancer" - (3) (三)
   "The research of XZ-C immunomodulation anticancer Chinese medications"
   ——Experimental research and clinical application verification

4. "Walked out of the new road to conquer cancer" – (4)(四)
   "Creating a Science City of Scientific Research Bases with Cancer Multidisciplinary and Cancer related research for conquering cancer"

5. "Walked out of the new road to conquer cancer" - (5)(五)
   "The Clinical Application Theory Innovation of 21ˢᵗ Century Cancer Prevention and Treatment Research"

6. "Walked out of the new road to conquer cancer" - (6)(六)
   XZ-C proposes <<to create the Cancer Prevention Research Institute of Environmental Protection >> and to carry out the system engineering of the cancer prevention
   ——Prevention of Pollution and Treatment and Control of Pollution and Prevention
       of cancer and Anti-cancer anti-cancer
   ——Dawning prevention cancer research plan and Dawning scientific research
       spirit
   ——Medical is benevolence and to set up the moral is the first

7. "Walk out of the new road to conquer cancer" - (7)(七)
   "Condense wisdom and conquer cancer - for the benefit of mankind" (part 1) and (part 2)

8. "Walked out of the new road to conquer cancer" - (8)(八)
   "The Road to overcome cancer"

The library of the medical research on Prevention of Cancer and Anti-cancer

The Collected Works of Professor Xu Ze (XZ-C)'s Research on Cancer Prevention and Cancer Treatment

XZ-C proposed: How to conquer cancer? How to prevent cancer? How to treat cancer?
XZ-C new concept of cancer treatment

Volume I
<<Conquer Cancer and Launch the total attack to cancer ———prevention cancer and cancer control and cancer treatment at the same level and at the same attention and at the same time>> *The book table or contents or directory (omitted)*

Volume II
<<Walked out of a new way of cancer treatment with the immune regulation and control of the combination of Chinese and Western medicine>> *The book table or contents or directory (omitted)*

Volume III
<<The research of XZ-C immunomodulation anticancer Chinese medicine ———Experimental research and clinical verification>> *The book table or contents or directory (omitted)*

Volume IV
<<To build the science base of multidisciplinary and cancer related research to overcome cancer-Science City>> *The book contents (omitted)*

Volume V
<<Theoretical Innovation of Cancer Prevention and Management or treatment cancer in the 21st Century>> *The book contents (Omitted)*

Volume VI
<<XZ-C proposes to create the preventing cancer research institute and to carry out a series of cancer prevention projects>> The book contents (Omitted)

Dawning C plan
Dawning A·B·D plan
Prevention of Cancer and Treatment of Cancer and Preventin of Cancer and anti-cancer
The Dawning Science Research Program
The Dawning Scientific research spirit
Doctor is benevolence, to set up the moral is first

Volume VII
<<Condense Wisdom and Conquer Cancer - Benefiting Mankind>> (Volume I and II, which book has two parts)
The book contents (Omitted)

Volume VIII
<<The Road to Overcome Cancer>> *The book contents (omitted)*

Volume IX
<<On Innovation of Treatment of Cancer>> *The book contents (omitted)*

Volume X
<<New understanding and new models of cancer treatment>> *The book contents (omitted)*

Volume XI
<<New Concepts and New Methods for Cancer Metastasis Treatment>> *The book Table of Contents (omitted)*

Volume XII
<<The New Progress in Cancer Treatment>> *Table of Contents (omitted)*

Volume XIII
"New Concepts and New Methods for Cancer Treatment" *The book table of contents (omitted)*

[Note: Each volume is a published monograph on cancer medical research]

Note:

1. **XZ-C is Xu Ze-China, because science is borderless, but scientists have national and intellectual property. 2 Cancer is a disaster for all mankind. It must evoke the struggle of the people all over the world. Therefore, there are 8 monographs in the series, which are all in English, distributed worldwide, and published on Amazon. com on barnesandnoble.com and on authorhouse.com.**

A Brief Introduction to The first Author

Xu Ze was born in 1933 in Leping City, Jiangxi Province, China. He graduated from Tongji Medical College in 1956. He served as the director of surgery, professor, chief physician, master and doctoral tutor of the Affiliated Hospital of Hubei College of Traditional Chinese Medicine. He is the director of the Experimental Surgery Research Institute of Hubei College of Traditional Chinese Medicine, director of the Department of Abdominal Oncology Surgery, and anti-cancer metastasis. Director of Recurrence Research Office; concurrently serves as executive director of Wuhan Branch of Chinese Medical Association, honorary president of Wuhan Anticancer Research Association, academic member of International Liver Disease Research Collaboration Center, member of International Federation of Surgeons, Chinese Journal of Experimental Surgery No. 1, 2, 3 The 4th Standing Editorial Board and the 1st, 2nd and 3rd Executive Editors of the Journal of Abdominal Surgery. He has been engaged in surgical work for 60 years and has extensive clinical experience in the surgical treatment of lung cancer, esophageal cancer, gastric cancer, liver cancer, gallbladder cancer, pancreatic cancer, and intestinal cancer, as well as the combination of Chinese and Western medicine to prevent postoperative recurrence and metastasis. In 1987, he began experimental research on tumors. Through cancer cell transplantation, he established tumor animal models, explored the mechanisms and rules of cancer metastasis and recurrence, and searched for ways to inhibit metastasis. Screening 48 kinds of natural drugs from anti-cancer invasion and metastasis And relapsed Chinese medicine, and based on this, developed xz-c immunomodulation anticancer traditional Chinese medicine preparation, clinically verified by a large number of cases, the effect is remarkable. Published 126 scientific research papers, published in 2001, "New Understanding and New Model of Cancer Treatment", published by Hubei Science and Technology Publishing House and published by Xinhua Bookstore. In 2006, he published the monograph "New Concept and New Method of Cancer Metastasis Treatment" published by Beijing People's Military Medical Publishing House and published by Xinhua Bookstore. In April 2007, he was awarded the original book award and certificate by the General Administration of Press and Publication of the People's Republic of China. In October 2011, the third monograph (New Concepts and New Methods of Cancer Treatment) was published by Beijing People's Military Medical Press. Xu Ze, Xu Jie/Zhang, Xinhua Bookstore was released. This book is translated into English by Dr. Bin Wu., published in Washington, DC on March 26, 2013, international distribution. He participated in 10 medical monographs such as "Hepatology Treatment" and "Abdominal Surgery". He engaged in teaching for 60 years, trained many young physicians, 10 master students And 2 doctoral students. He has been engaged in surgical research for 34 years and has achieved many results. Among them, "self-made xz-c: type abdominal cavity-venous bypass device for the treatment of cirrhotic refractory ascites and its clinical application" was awarded the Hubei Provincial Government Science and Technology for the second prize of the results, and promoted and applied in 38 hospitals across the country: The National Natural Science Foundation of China's experimental study on the pathophysiology and pathogenesis of pulmonary schistosomiasis by experimental surgical methods won the second prize of Hubei Provincial Government Science and Technology Achievements. He enjoys Special government allowance.

A Brief Introduction to the Second Author

Xu Jie, male, graduated from Hubei College of Traditional Chinese Medicine in 1992, graduated from Hubei Medical University in 1996, Department of Clinical Medicine. Now He is chief physician in Hubei University of Traditional Chinese Medicine Hospital and Hubei Provincial Hospital of Surgery, engaged in experimental surgical tumor research and general surgery, urology clinical work.

Since 1992, he has been involved in the experimental tumor research of the Institute of Experimental Surgery of Hubei College of Traditional Chinese Medicine. He has carried out cancer cell transplantation and established a tumor animal model. He has carried out a series of experimental tumor research: exploring the mechanism of recurrence and metastasis of cancer and in vivo screening experiment of more than 200 kinds of Chinese herbal medicine in vivo tumor model of tumor inhibition s from a large number of natural medicine to find out, screening out of 48 kinds of anti-cancer invasion, metastasis, relapse traditional Chinese medicine

He participates in clinical validation and followed up for XZ - C immunoregulatory Chinese herbal medicine and completes the experimental research and clinical verification, data collection, collection and summary of this book.

A brief introduction to the third author and the main translator and the main editor

Bin Wu, MD, Ph.D., graduated from College of Yunyang of Tongji University of Medical Sciences for her MD degree; Studied her Master degree and her Ph. D degree in Sun Yat-Sen University of Medical Sciences. After she received her Ph.D., she worked as a Post-doctoral Follews in the Johns Hopkins Medical School and University of Maryland Medical School. She passed her USMLE tests and is going to do her residency training in America. She dedicated herself to oncology clinical and research. Her goal is to conquer cancer, which she believes this great contribution to our health. She has a daughter, named Lily Xu who drew all of the pictures in this book.

A Brief introduction to the illustrator and the advisor

Lily Xu was born on November 17th 2006 and had an art presented in the Walter Art Museum in Baltimore at the age of 6; she got the fourth place trophy in the ES Double Digits or 24 and 24 games in the Baltimore County in Maryland; she got the first trophy in the BCPS STEM FAIR PHYSICS in Baltimore County; when she was in the sixth grade, she passed the advanced Math for 7th grade(which means the 8th grade math) test and moved the 8th grade math class; she loves the reading and the writing and she finished many series of books. She got $6000 scholarship award for the Peabody music program in the Johns Hopkins University. In 2018 she was chosen into Baltimore county Middle school Honor Band. In 2018 the robotic team which she attended for years got designing-award from the Baltimore county so that this robotic team will come to Maryland State for the Robotic contest. On January 19th, 2019 she got the Robotic designing-award in Maryland. She edits all of my books for the publishing and drew all of the pictures in this book.

Acknowledgements

This book is for all of people who concern human being health. We are deeply grateful to all of people who like our new ways to improve our human being health.

My daughter **Lily Xu** gave me many smart and creative ideas while we were finishing this book. Lily Xu drew all of the pictures such as the Thymus etc. **The characteristics of she loves the challenge** and **her judgment always encourages me to continue working hard to move on**.

I would like to express our sincere gratitude to the following:

1. All of Authorhouse staffs
2. Dr. Xu Ze's family and Dr. Xu Jie's family, especially his son Zihao Xu, who is the medical student in China
3. Mrs. Bo Wu's family and Mrs. Tao Wu's famly: espeicaly their daughters Chongshu Luo and Xunyue Wang

Bin Wu, M.D., Ph.D
01-28-2019 in Baltimore, Maryland in USA

Introduction (1)

1. **Characteristics of traditional Chinese medicine immunopharmacology**

Immunopharmacology is an interdisciplinary subject that combines immunology with pharmacology. It has a long history and is progressing rapidly.

Traditional Chinese medicine immunopharmacology can be understood as a new discipline combining traditional Chinese medicine with modern immunopharmacology. Traditional Chinese medication is a medication applied under the guidance of traditional Chinese medicine theory. The application and research of traditional Chinese medication cannot be separated from the guidance of traditional Chinese medicine theory. **Therefore, the research on the immune pharmacology of traditional Chinese medicine which is carried out is to study how to combine the theory of traditional Chinese medicine with the ideas and methods of modern immunology, and to carry out immunopharmacological research combining Chinese and Western medicine.**

TCM theory has its obvious overall view, emphasizing the balance of the body. The reason why the normal body can balance when the internal and external environment changes is to depend on the balance of yin and yang, the coordination of gas and blood, viscera organs, internal organs and meridians, etc. When the body has loss of balance and coordination, the body will have the disease symptoms. Clinical syndrome differentiation and treatment are inseparable from the overall view, which is inseparable from macroeconomic regulation and control, and finally achieves the recovery of the body.

Modern medicine also emphasizes the stability of the internal environment. The regulatory factors for the stability in the internal environment are the three systems of nerve, endocrine and immunity. These are both self-contained systems, independently play their respective regulatory roles, and at the same time they are interconnected and interact with each other to achieve the goal of maintaining a relatively stable internal environment. The "Neuroendocrine Immunoregulatory Network" (NIM network) is currently a research hotspot in immunopharmacology.

Ancient Chinese medicine has been having the concepts and theory that while there is righteous spirit or right things, the evil spirits cannot enter into the body or win the body war, which forms a theoretical component of Chinese medicine and It has a series of prescriptions for strengthening the body and replenishing the vital energy and developing the tonic medicine. Its essence is to regulate qi and blood and yin and yang, maintain the overall functional balance, and enhance disease resistance**. In modern scientific language, the main role of tonic drugs is to enhance the body's immune function**. It can be seen that the tonic drugs or the medications with the supplement of the body benefits are based on immunology and immunopharmacology.

In the 1970s, a large number of internationally reported thymus were the "central organs" of the immune system, producing immune cells and transporting them to the body to exert immunomodulatory effects. As early as the late 1970s, Professor Zhou Jin in China called for the establishment of pharmacology in the integration of Chinese and Western medicine in China. It was proposed to study and clarify the pharmacology of traditional Chinese medication from the theory of traditional Chinese medicine. They have done a lot of groundbreaking and exploratory research, studied the relationship between Chinese medication and immunopharmacology and its potential huge vitality, and made gratifying progress.

Immunopharmacology is a new discipline combining immunology with pharmacology. Its formation is one of several new disciplines along with the development of Modern biology and basic medical science, in which these include new discoveries in immunology, such as thymosin, immune cells, and immune factors, etc.

The general goal of immunopharmacology can be summarized as **the use of various means and drugs to regulate the function of the immune system so that the endogenous immune response produces beneficial effects on the patient's body**.

Immunopharmacology entered the preclinical immunopharmaceutical testing of immunotherapy since the mid-1970s. In 1979, the English "Immunopharmacology" textbook was officially published. The main contents include inflammatory immunology, immunosuppressive therapy, cyclic nucleotide pharmacology, and immunotherapy, etc. Immunopharmacology has officially become one of the internationally recognized emerging disciplines. The International Society of Immunopharmacology was formally established in 1983 as a specialist association of the International Society of Pharmacology.

China's immunology and immunopharmacology are also developing rapidly. In the early 1980s, there were publications "Immunopharmacology", "Chinese Medication and Immunity", "Chinese Medication Immunity", "Chinese Medication Immunopharmacology", in which have a special chapter on traditional Chinese medication tonic drugs, with immune regulation as the central idea. Traditional Chinese medication immunopharmacology plays an important role in the pharmacology of traditional Chinese medicine.

2. Why study Chinese medicine immunopharmacology

In 1985, I conducted a petition with more than 3,000 patients who had undergone radical resection of various cancers. It was found that most patients relapsed and metastasized 2 to 3 years after surgery, and some even metastasized several months after surgery. This makes me realize that although the operation is successful, the long-term efficacy is not satisfactory. Postoperative recurrence and metastasis are the key factors affecting the long-term efficacy of the operation. It also reminds us that prevention and treatment of postoperative recurrence and metastasis is the key to prolonging postoperative survival. Therefore, basic research must be carried out, and without breakthroughs in basic research, clinical efficacy is difficult to improve.

Thus, in October 1985, we established an experimental surgical research laboratory and conducted the following series of animal experiments.

(1) **New findings in our laboratory research:**

    1. Excision of the thymus can produce a cancer-bearing animal model.

    2. Experimental results suggest that metastasis is related to immunity, and immune function is low, which can promote cancer metastasis.

    3. The experimental results showed that the host thymus was acutely progressively atrophied after inoculation of cancer cells, and the proliferation of thymocytes was blocked and the size or volume of Thymus has shrunk or reduced significantly.

    4. The experimental results showed that when the experimental mice were inoculated with cancer cells and the solid tumor grows to a large thumb, it is removed. After one week, the thymus did not undergo progressive atrophy on the anatomical discovery.

From the results of our laboratory experiments above it is found that:

The thymus of the cancer-bearing mice showed progressive atrophy, the volume was reduced, the cell proliferation was blocked, the mature cells were reduced, and the immune function was low. By the end of the tumor, the thymus is extremely atrophied and the texture becomes hard. Therefore, it is necessary to prevent thymic atrophy, immune regulation and control, and immune reconstitution.

(2) **Therefore, XZ-C proposes that the treatment of cancer must take a new path of treatment of cancer with immune regulation and control. So how should I perform immunomodulatory therapy? We are looking for both western medicine and traditional Chinese medication.**

    1. Western medicine can increase the immunity of drugs rarely

    2. Chinese medicine has a large number of prescriptions that have the function of regulating immune function, especially the beneficial effects of traditional Chinese medicines on regulating immune activity.

(3) **So our laboratory conducted an experimental study on screening the medications with anti-cancer, metastasis, and increasing immune function from traditional Chinese medication:**

    1. Adopting in vitro culture of cancer cells to conduct screening experiments on the rate of cancer suppression in Chinese herbal medicine

        a. in vitro screening test

        b. in-tube screening test

2. Manufacture of cancer-bearing animal models, and experimental screening of Chinese herbal medicines for cancer suppression rate in cancer-bearing animals

The whole group of mice were inoculated with EAS or S_{180} or H_{22} cancer cells to produce a cancer-bearing animal model. 5-F or CTX was used as the control group. Each rat was orally fed with crude bio-powder, and the traditional Chinese medicine was screened for long-term feeding. The survival time, toxicity and side effects, calculation of prolonged survival rate and calculation of cancer inhibition rate were observed.

Experimental results:

Among the 200 Chinese herbal medicines screened by animal experiments in our laboratory, 48 strains which have a good inhibitory effect on cancer cell proliferation were selected, and the tumor inhibition rate was 75-90%.

(4) 48 traditional Chinese medicines that have been screened out from this experiment and have a good tumor inhibition rate were combined optimized, and then the vivo inhibition tests were repeated and it finally consisted of $XZ-C_{1-10}$ (Xu Ze-China) immunomodulatory anti-cancer series of traditional Chinese medicine preparations. It has been applied to clinical practice on the basis of the success of animal experiments. After more than 12,000 clinical cases in 34 years, it has been clinically proven and the effective results are excellent.

(5) **Therefore, we first proposed at the international level:**

1. Walked out of the new path of conquering cancer of the combination of Chinese and Western medicine at the molecular lever with traditional Chinese medicine immune regulation and control, regulate immune activity, prevent thymus atrophy, promote thymic hyperplasia, protect the bone marrow hematopoietic function and improve immune surveillance.
2. The theoretical system of XZ-C cancer treatment has been formed, which is the theoretical basis and experimental basis for treatment of cancer with immune regulation and control, is undergoing clinical application observation verification.
3. We have walked out of the new way of cancer treatment with XZ-C immune regulation and control of the combination of Chinese and Western medicine at the molecular level--- - the "Chinese style anti-cancer" new road.
4. A series of products of researched and developed XZ-C anti-cancer with the immune regulation and control

Many Chinese herbal medicines are immune enhancers, biological response modifiers, tonics, and many of them can strengthen the body's immunity and anti-cancer function.

At present, scientists around the world agree that tumor formation is summarized into three processes:

In the first step, carcinogenic factors act on the body and interfere with cell metabolism;
The second step is to disrupt the genetic information in the nucleus and cause cancer of the

cell; The third step is that the cancer cells escape the body's immune alert defense system, and the body's immune defense ability is an internal cause. The external factors must be functioned through the internal factors. Cancer cells must be able to escape the body's alarm system surveillance, break through the body's immune defense, in order to develop into a tumor. Therefore, trying to improve the body's immunity is the key measures to preventing cancer and treating cancer. Chinese herbal medicine is an extremely important advantage, and there are many immune Chinese herbal preparations, which there is a rich source of medicine, which should be used as an important anti-cancer and anti-cancer resource. It should be organized for research and development.

In the field of cancer research, traditional Chinese medication is China's advantage, and this advantage is studied. It should be a strategic vision of international significance.

To study, discover and develop effective and repeatable new anti-cancer and anti-cancer Chinese herbal preparations, strict scientific methods must be used. Modern experimental surgical methods, the effective components of immune regulation and anti-cancer Chinese medicine, molecular level analysis and research, gene level experimental research, first separate the active ingredients, so that the precious heritage of traditional Chinese medicine is modernized and scientific.

Strict, objective, and realistic research on scientific and repeated verification must be carried out using rigorous scientific methods. Investigate, must pass rigorous clinical verification, in a large number of patients, the evidence is clear that there is a good effect, the standard of evaluation of efficacy is that the patient's quality of life is good, the survival period is significantly prolonged, complications are no or less.

Traditional Chinese medication pharmacy is the essence of Chinese culture. One of the essence of traditional medicine is Chinese medicatoin pharmacy, and the traditional Chinese medication is clinically effective on the basis of the substance contained in the chemical composition. To study the anti-tumor effect and mechanism of traditional Chinese medication, it is necessary to study the active ingredients in depth so that it makes the precious heritage of traditional medicine in China tends to be more modern and scientific.

Introduction (2)

In the 1970s, there was a large number of international reports that the thymus was the "central organ" of the immune system, producing immune cells and transporting them to the body to exert immunomodulatory effects.

As early as the late 1970s, Professor Zhou Jin of China called for the establishment of pharmacology in the integration of Chinese and Western medicine in China, and did a lot of groundbreaking and exploratory research, and studied and clarified the pharmacology of traditional Chinese medicine from the theory of traditional Chinese medicine and achieved promising progress.

In 1979, the English "Immunopharmacology" textbook was officially published, and immunopharmacology became one of the internationally recognized emerging disciplines.

In 1983, the International Society of Immunopharmacology officially became a special science society of the International Society of Pharmacology.

Since 1985, I have written to more than 3,000 cases of chest and abdominal cancer. It was found that most patients relapsed or metastasized within 2-3 years after surgery, and some even relapsed and metastasized and died within 1 year after surgery.

From the results of the follow-up, it was found:

1. Postoperative recurrence and metastasis are the key factors affecting the long-term efficacy of surgery.Therefore, we also raised an important issue: the study of prevention and treatment of cancer recurrence and metastasis is the key to improve the long-term efficacy of surgery. It is the key to improve the survival of patients after surgery.
2. Therefore, clinical basic research to prevent cancer recurrence and metastasis must be carried out. Without breakthroughs in basic research, clinical efficacy is difficult to improve.

So in October 1985, we established an experimental surgical laboratory (formerly known as surgical liver ascites laboratory, laboratory equipment is better) to conduct experimental tumor research, perform cancer cell transplantation, establish a tumor animal model, and carried out a series of Experimental tumor research. Until March 8, 1991, it was founded the Institute of Experimental Surgery, Hubei College of Traditional Chinese Medicine; Professor Xu Ze is the director of the institute, and Professor and the academician Qiu Fazu is the consultant of the institute which took the 'conquer cancer' as the research direction. With the research direction of "conquering cancer", a series of experimental tumor research work was carried out:

A. Explored the mechanism and regularity of cancer recurrence and metastasis;
B. Explored the relationship between tumors and immune and immune organs and immune organs and tumors;
C. Discussed methods for suppressing progressive atrophy of immune organs and rebuilding immunity when tumor progression is inhibited;
D. Found effective measures to regulate and to control cancer invasion, recurrence, and metastasis;
E. Screened of anti-cancer Chinese herbal medicines commonly used in 200 literatures for the anti-tumor experiment of animal models of solid tumors;
F. Explored new drugs from anti-cancer, anti-metastatic and anti-recurrence drugs from natural medicines, and 48 kinds of XZ-C1-10 immunomodulatory anticancer Chinese medicines with good curative effect were screened out.
G. Applied to clinical practice on the basis of the success of animal experiments. After 24 years of clinical application of a large number of clinical cases (more than 12,000 cases), the curative effect is remarkable.

In October 1985, we established an experimental surgery laboratory in our clinical surgery to conduct research on experimental tumors.

The tumor model was examined and began to move from clinical to basic experimental research.

1. **Experimental study on manufacturing cancer animal models**

At the time, the author was the director of clinical surgery and director of the experimental surgery research department of the Affiliated Hospital of Hubei College of Traditional Chinese Medicine, which facilitated the coordination of the work of clinical wards and animal laboratories, and synchronized and coordinated, we did not have any experience in manufacturing cancer animal models at the time. The "bone graft" method was used for allogeneic transplantation of cancer tissues, and the sterile tumor specimens were taken from the clinical operating table. The warm ischemia was transplanted to the experimental animals for 0.5 h, and more than 100 times (400 animals) were performed. None of them succeeded.

A lot of international reports in the late 1970s, the thymus is the "central organ" of the immune system, producing immune cells that are transported throughout the body to exert immunomodulatory effects.

Among long-term use of hormones, cortisone treatment of chronic patients with low immune function, the incidence of cancer is higher.

At the beginning of 1987, our surgical laboratory removed the thymus and re-transplanted the mouse, and it was successful (210 animals). Some of them were injected with cortisone, which reduced the immunity of the mice. It was also transplantable successfully. The thymus was removed for 5 days. After -6 days, the soy bean-size nodules can grow, 10-21d long to the big tumor of the thumb, and the transplanted cancer can survive for 3-4 weeks, but it cannot be passaged.

Through this research, it is found that:

(1) Excision of the thymus can produce a model of a cancer-bearing animal, and injection of cortisone also contributes to the production of a cancer-bearing animal model.

(2) The research conclusions prove that the occurrence and development of cancer is related to the host's immunity. It has a very obvious relationship with the function of immune organs.

(3) The results of this study confirmed that the immune system thymus (Thymus, Th) and immune function have a very definite relationship with the occurrence and development of cancer. If the host thymus is removed, it may be a cancer-bearing animal model. Without resection, it cannot cause a cancer-bearing animal model. Injecting an immunosuppressive drug to reduce host immunity can help to produce a cancer-bearing animal model, and cannot produce a cancer-bearing animal model without injecting a reduced immunological drug.

This result indicates that immune organs and immunity are negatively correlated with cancer cell transplantation, implantation and growth into solid cancer. When there is Immunodeficiency or immune reduction, the transplant can grow a tumor out of the bed and will not be swallowed by the host's immune cell recognition.

2. Experimental study on manufacturing the model of cancer metastasis

Regarding cancer cell transplantation research, in 1987, the author conducted dozens of human cancer cells transplanted into the thymus-free mice in the experimental surgery laboratory. A solid cancer transplantation model was established.

(1) Later, a cancer metastasis model was made.

To simulate **lymphatic metastasis and establish** an animal model of experimental lymphatic metastasis, we transplanted 106/ml, 0.2 ml of H22 cell suspension subcutaneously on the inner side of 60 mouse paw pads. After 7-8d, the inside of the paw pad grew a large tumor of broad bean, and the entire ankle was swollen and wrapped. After 16 days, in 8 mice it was found the swollen right abdomen lymph node and established a lymphatic metastasis model.

(2) After that, the mode of the **simulated blood metastasis** was set up.

H22 cell suspension 106/ml, 0.4ml was injected into mice intravenously, and more lung metastasis was obtained, which caused tumor growth in the lung, and an experimental lung metastasis animal model was established.

(3) Afterwards, we established an animal model of **experimental liver metastasis** in our laboratory.

Eighty Kunming mice were divided into two groups, A and B, 40 in each group. Group A was injected with cortisone for 7 days, and all were anesthetized by intraperitoneal injection of 1% pentobarbital 75 mg/kg. Then in the left middle abdomen it made a 0.5cm long incision, exposed the spleen, and took the living body H22 liver cancer ascites 10ul to give spleen subcapsular injection. Local compression for 3-5 minutes was done to prevent cancer cells from spilling out into the abdominal cavity, and the cancer cells injected under the spleen envelope slowly enter the lymph and blood. After the animals were reared for 11 days, the neck was killed and the liver was taken for colony colony counting.

RESULTS: There were cancer metastasis in the liver of mice in group A and group B. The number of intrahepatic metastases was different. The number of group A was significantly higher than that of group B, mostly 3-5 or more, and the diameter was about 1mm. It is 1-3.

The experimental results suggest that metastasis is clearly related to immunization, immune function is low, or drugs that suppress immunity can be used to promote tumor metastasis.

On March 8, 1991, we established the Institute of Experimental Surgery. And from the following 3 aspects, it spent 34 years to conduct a series of experimental studies and clinical validation work.

First, explored the mechanisms of cancer onset, invasion and recurrence and metastasis.

It was carried out experimental research on effective measures to regulate invasion, recurrence and metastasis. We have carried out a full 4 years of research on cancer experiments in the laboratory, which is the basis for clinical basic research and all of the research projects were clinically raised questions. It is intended to explain these clinical problems or solve these clinical problems through experimental research.

Second, Experimental Study of looking for new anti-cancer, anti-metastatic, anti-relapse drugs from natural medicines.

The existing anticancer drugs kill both cancer cells and normal cells, and have large adverse reactions. We used anti-tumor experiments in cancer-bearing mice to find new drugs that inhibit cancer cells without affecting normal cells. We spent a full three years on the anti-tumor screening experiments of cancer-bearing animals in 200 kinds of Chinese herbal medicines used in traditional anti-cancer prescriptions and anti-cancer agents reported in various places. RESULTS: 48 kinds of traditional Chinese medicines with good anti-tumor effect and good effects were screened out, and the traditional Chinese medicine Huang Lateng ethyl acetate extract (TG) which can inhibit the new microvessels was found out.

Third, clinical validation work

Through the above four years to explore the basic experimental research of recurrence and metastasis mechanism, and after three years of experimental research screening from natural drugs, a group of XZ-C1-10 immunomodulatory anticancer Chinese medicines were identified, and the clinical validation of more than 12,000 patients with advanced or postoperative metastatic cancer in 20 years was applied. XZ-C immunomodulation of anticancer Chinese medicine was achieved. The effect can improve the quality of life of patients, improve the symptoms of patients, and significantly prolong the survival of patients.

Through the review, analysis, reflection and experience of my clinical practice cases for more than 60 years, combined with the results and findings of my more than 34 years of experimental research on tumor-bearing animals, I published a new understanding of cancer treatment in January 2001 by Hubei Science and Technology Press. And the new model>, published in January 2006 by the People's Medical Publishing House, "New Concepts and New Methods for Cancer Metastasis Treatment", which was also awarded "Three by the General Administration of Press and Publication of the People's Republic of China" in April 2007. One hundred "Original Book Award. These monographs are a true record of scientific thinking from "experiment to clinical, then clinical to experimental." The summary of experimental research and clinical verification data has risen to the theoretical essence, and new discoveries and new understandings have been proposed, such as clinical practical oncology theory, cancer treatment, research development and reform, and these clinical practical innovation theories can be used to guide Clinical treatment work.

The theoretical innovation of carrying out the clinical application is because all clinical treatment, medication, and diagnosis must have a reasonable theoretical basis. More than 60 years of clinical oncology practice has made me deeply understand that because the etiology, pathogenesis and pathophysiology of tumors are not well understood. More than 60 years of clinical oncology practice has made me realize that because the etiology, pathogenesis and pathophysiology of tumors are not well understood, "oncology" has become one of the most backward developments in medical science. More basic scientific research, clinical validation research, and a combination of basic and clinical research are needed.

In the past 7 years, a series of clinical basic experimental research and basic problems have been explored on more than 6,000 tumor-bearing animal models. The screening of 200 kinds of Chinese herbal medicines in the tumor-bearing animal model has been screened in vivo. These were completed by several graduate students. "Exploring the effect of spleen on tumor growth and the anti-cancer effect of Jianpi Yiqi Decoction" was completed by Master Zhu Siping: "Experimental study on the combined transplantation of fetal liver, spleen and thymocytes for the treatment of malignant tumors by Zong Shaomin" The Ph.D. completed: "Experimental study on the anti-tumor effect of Fuzheng Peiben on S180 mice" was completed by Master Li Zhengxun; "Experimental study on the inhibitory effect of ethyl acetate extract (TG) on the neovascularization of transplanted tumors in mice", Completed by Liu Wei Master. The subjects of the master's and doctoral students are the sub-topics of my total research project, and they are the basic issues closely related to clinical practice. The graduate students have carried out and completed a lot of hard and meticulous experimental research work, contributing to the development of anti-cancer, anti-cancer and experimental oncology medicine.

Guidance

How to overcome cancer, how to prevent cancer by I see
How can I treat cancer by I see

XZ-C found problems and raised problems from follow-up results (Hint: how to prevent postoperative recurrence and metastasis is the key to improve long-term outcomes after surgery)
↓

Pathfinding *(to overcome cancer, where is the road? How do you find it?)*
↓

Pathfinding and footprint *(the series of the scientific research results and scientific and technological innovation of cancer prevention and anti-cancer metastasis research)*
↓

Published cancer monographs *(3 Chinese editions are exclusively distributed nationwide, 5 full English editions are published worldwide)*
↓

Participated in the International Congress of Oncology (AACR Academic Conference in USA)
↓

Visited the Stirling Cancer Institute in Houston, USA (2009)
↓

Accumulated Basic and clinical research on prevention of cancer and anti-cancer metastasis in the past more than 60 years
↓

Accumulated the clinical application experience from more than 12,000 cases in the past more than 34 years
↓

Walked Out of the new road to treat cancer with an immune regulatory and control of the combination of Chinese and Western medicine at the molecular level

---**Walked out of the new road of conquering cancer**
---**Published the English monograph "The Road to Overcome Cancer"** in December 6, 2016, published in Washington, DC, global distribution, Amazon website and Barnesandnoble.com and Authorhouse.com

---**Published the English monograph "Condense Wisdom and Conquer Cancer"** in December 2017 (volume 1), published in February 2018 (the next volume), published in Washington, USA, full English version, global distribution, Amazon website and Barnesandnoble. com and Authorhouse.com.

---Published the English monograph **"Conquer Cancer and launch The Total Attack to Cancer"** – cancer prevention and cancer control and cancer treatment at the same level and at the same attention) In November 2018, the United States published in Washington, DC, and the Amazon website and Barnesandnoble.com and Authorhouse.com

Foreword (1)

The prospect of immunomodulatory drugs is gratifying.

Regardless of the complexity of the mechanisms behind cancer, immune suppression is the key to cancer progression. Removing the immunosuppressive factor and restoring the recognition of cancer cells by systemic cells can effectively prevent cancer. More and more research evidence shows that by regulating the body's immune system, it is possible to achieve the goal of controlling cancer. Treating tumors by activating the body's anti-tumor immune system is an area that is currently exciting for researchers. A major breakthrough in the next cancer is likely to stem from this.

In order to explore the etiology, pathogenesis and pathophysiology of cancer, we conducted a series of animal experiments. From the analysis of experimental results, we obtained new findings and new enlightenments: thymus atrophy and low immune function are one of the causes and pathogenesis of cancer. Therefore, Professor Xu Ze proposed at the international conference that one of the causes and pathogenesis of cancer may be thymus atrophy and impaired central immune sensory function and Immune function is low and reduced immune surveillance and immune escape.

As a result of laboratory experiments, it was found that the thymus of the cancer-bearing mice showed progressive atrophy and the central immune sensory function was impaired. The immune function is reduced and the immune surveillance is low, so the treatment principle must be to prevent progressive atrophy of the thymus and promote thymic hyperplasia. Protecting bone marrow hematopoietic function enhances immune surveillance and provides a theoretical basis and experimental basis for immune regulation and treatment of cancer.

Based on the above findings on the experimental results of cancer etiology and pathogenesis, it is a new concept and new method for XZ-C immunomodulation therapy. After 34years of oncology clinic outpatients more than 12,000 cases of patients with advanced cancer, clinical validation observations confirmed that the principle of treatment of protecting Thymus and increasing immune function or immune function enhancement is reasonable and satisfactory. The application of immunomodulatory Chinese medicine has achieved good results, improved the quality of life, and significantly prolonged the survival period.

<u>XZ-C (XU ZE-China) immune regulation and control was first proposed by Professor Xu Ze in his book "New Concepts and New Methods of Cancer Metastasis Treatment" in 2006. He believes that under normal circumstances, there is a dynamic balance between</u>

cancer and body defense, and the occurrence of cancer is caused by a dynamic imbalance. If the condition that has been dysregulated is adjusted to a normal level, the growth of the cancer can be controlled and allowed to subside.

As we all know, the occurrence, development and prognosis of cancer are determined by the comparison of two factors, namely the biological characteristics and cancer of cancer cells. The host body itself has the ability to control the cancer cells. If the two balance, the cancer can be controlled. If the two are unbalanced, the cancer develops.

Under normal circumstances, the host's body itself has certain restraining ability on cancer cells, but in the case of cancer, these restrictive defense capabilities are inhibited and damaged to varying degrees, resulting in cancer cells losing immune surveillance and cancer cell immune escape to make cancer cells develop and metastasize further.

Through the above four years to explore the basic experimental research on the mechanism of recurrence and metastasis, and in addition after 3 years, from the natural experiment of natural Chinese herbal medicine, the antitumor test was carried out in mice bearing cancer. A batch of traditional Chinese medicines with good tumor inhibition rate were selected from Chinese herbal medicines to form XZ-C$_{1-10}$ anti-cancer immune regulation Chinese medicine.

Foreword (2)

Experimental surgery is extremely important in the development of medicine. It is a key to opening the medical exclusion zone. Many disease prevention methods have been studied in many animal experiments, and the stability results have been applied to the clinic to promote the development of the medical cause.

Developing science and technological innovation, the laboratory is the key condition. I deeply understand the importance of the laboratory. I am the first batch of college students in the post-liberation college entrance examination. I have not studied for extra school or academics or studied abroad, but I have achieved many international achievements. The key is that I have a good laboratory.

In the 1960s, I participated in the open heart surgery laboratory for cardiopulmonary bypass. In the 1980s, I established a cirrhosis ascites laboratory. In the 1990s, I established the Institute of Experimental Surgery to focus on cancer. In my animal laboratory, equipment conditions are good, there are mouse, rabbit, Dutch pig, rabbit, dog, monkey and other animal experiments, there is a better sterilization operating room. It can be used for chest and abdomen major surgery and animal postoperative observation room. It can bring various designs, ideas and experiments to achieve results or conclusions.

Therefore, the laboratory is the key condition, and the key is to build a good equipment laboratory. There should be a dual task on the shoulders of university teachers. One is to do a good job of teaching; the other is to develop science.

University teachers should have good laboratories for scientific research. Follow the scientific development concept, based on known science, explore unknown science, Future-oriented science, Emerging disciplines, marginal disciplines, interdisciplinary subjects, facing the frontiers of science, striving for innovation and progress, adding to the science hall.

In summary, experimental research and basic research are very important. Without experimental research and breakthroughs in basic research, clinical efficacy is difficult to improve, and it is difficult to propose new understandings, new concepts, and new theoretical insights. Among them, the experiment is the key. I have a good laboratory. I am the director of the Institute of Experimental Surgery and the director of clinical surgery. The experimental research, basic research and clinical verification are convenient for overall planning.

Basic research in medicine is very important for achieving progress in combating disease. Experimental oncology is the basic science of cancer prevention research. It has promoted the continuous development of cancer research in China. Our Institute of Experimental Surgery has conducted a series of experimental studies to explore the mechanisms of cancer onset, invasion and recurrence and metastasis. The laboratory conducted a full 4 years of research on cancer experiments, and found from experimental tumor research: Thymus atrophy, immune function is low, may be the cause of tumor, one of the pathogenesis, how to prevent thymus atrophy? How to regulate immune function is low? How to promote immunity? How to "protect Thymus and enhance the immune function "? Immune regulation and control should be carried out, and the combination of Western medicine and Chinese at the molecular level should be performed. It walked out of a new road with Chinese characteristics to overcome cancer.

Face the future of medicine, look forward, after 60 years of hard work, practice the scientific concept of development, face the frontiers of science, and strive for innovation and progress. To conquer cancer, it must be from the clinical, through experimental research, to the clinic to solve the actual problems of patients; Must be realistic, use facts, speak with data; Must constantly self-transcend, self-advance; In scientific research, we should emancipate our minds, break away from traditional old ideas, stand on independent innovation, and original innovation. Our decades of research are to discover problems → ask questions → study problems → solve problems or explain problems. The road is like this, step by step, difficult to travel, we hope to walk out of an innovative road with anti-cancer and anti-transfer with Chinese characteristics and independent intellectual property rights.

Our research model for oncology is based on patients, discovering and asking questions from clinical work, conducting in-depth basic research on animal experiments, and then turning basic research results into clinical applications to improve the overall level of medical care and ultimately benefit patients.

1

Overview of XZ-C immunomodulation of anticancer Chinese medication

A. Formation process of Experimental study and clinical validation of the new way to treat cancer by immunomodulation of traditional Chinese medications

(1) From follow-up to establishment of experimental surgical laboratory

Since 1985, the author has conducted a petition to more than 3,000 patients who have undergone chest and abdominal cancer surgery. All patients relapsed or metastasized in 2 to 3 years, and some even relapsed and metastasized and died after several months and 1 year after surgery.

These patients are often not returned to the original surgical surgery after surgery, but to the oncology or cancer hospital for radiotherapy and chemotherapy.

- Through large-scale follow-up, the author found an important issue, that is, postoperative recurrence and metastasis are the key factor of the long-term effects of surgery.
- Therefore, we also recognize that research on prevention and treatment of cancer recurrence and metastasis is the key to improving the long-term efficacy of surgery. It is the key to improve the survival of patients after surgery.
- Therefore, clinicians must conduct clinical basic research to prevent cancer recurrence and metastasis. If there is no breakthrough in basic research, then Clinical efficacy is difficult to improve.

Based on the follow-up results, the next research goals were determined:

1. In order to prevent postoperative recurrence and metastasis, to improve postoperative long-term treatment, the effective basic clinical research must be conducted;
2. In order to study prevention of recurrence and metastasis, experimental tumor models must be established for experimental research.

1

Therefore, we established an experimental surgical laboratory to conduct experimental tumor research, perform cancer cell transplantation, and establish a tumor animal model type, conducted a series of experimental tumor research.

- Explore the mechanism and regularity of cancer recurrence and metastasis, and explore the relationship between tumors and immune and immune organs, as well as immune organs and tumors.
- Explored ways to suppress progressive atrophy of immune organs and re-immunize when tumor progression.
- Looked for effective measures to regulate cancer invasion, recurrence, and metastasis.
- Screening of 200 anti-cancer Chinese herbal medicines commonly used in the literature for the anti-tumor rate of cancer-bearing solid tumors.
- Explored the anti-cancer, anti-metastatic, anti-recurrence new drugs from natural medication using modern science and technology and in-depth study and discover the anti-cancer and anti-cancer Chinese herbal medications.
- Strict and scientific and repeated screening of tumor-inhibiting rate in cancer-bearing animal models from the traditionally recognized anti-cancer Chinese herbal medications; eliminated the medications with the unstable effects; 48 kinds of XZ-C immunomodulatory anti-tumor drugs with good curative effect were screened out.
- Based on the success of animal experiments, applied to clinical practice. After 12 years of clinical trials of a large number of clinical cases, the effect is remarkable.

(2) new discoveries

1. Found from the results of follow-up

   (1) Postoperative recurrence and metastasis are the key factors affecting the long-term efficacy of surgery, so we also raised an important issue, namely clinicians must pay attention to and study the prevention and treatment of postoperative recurrence and metastasis in order to improve the long-term efficacy of postoperative.

   (2) Clinical basic research on recurrence and metastasis must be carried out. Without breakthroughs in basic research, clinical efficacy is difficult to improve.

2. Found from experimental tumor research

   (1) Excision of the thymus can produce a model of cancer-bearing animals, and injection of immunosuppressive drugs can also contribute to the establishment of a cancer-bearing animal model.

   The conclusions of the study clearly demonstrate that the occurrence and development of cancer and the host's immune organ thymus and the tissue function of the immune organ are clear relationship.

(2) The question is that Whether it is that First immunization is low and then easy to get cancer, or it is that getting cancer first and then getting low immunity, our experimental results are that First, there is a low level of immunity and then easy to have the occurrence and development of cancer. If there is no decline in immune function, it is not easy to be vaccinated successfully.

The results suggest that improving and maintaining good immune function protects the thymus of the immune organ is one of the important measures to prevent cancer.

(3) When studying the relationship between metastasis and immunity of cancer, an animal model of liver metastasis was established, divided into two groups, A and B, and group A was immunized with the Inhibition drug, group B is not used. The result was that the number of intrahepatic metastases in group A was significantly greater than in group B.

The experimental results suggest that metastasis is associated with immunity, low immune function or the use of immunosuppressive drugs to promote tumor metastasis.

(4) When investigating the effect of tumor on immune organs, it was found that the thymus was progressively atrophy as the cancer progressed.

Immediately after inoculation of cancer cells, the thymus of the host showed acute progressive atrophy, cell proliferation was blocked, and the volume was significantly reduced.

The experimental results suggest that the tumor will inhibit the thymus and cause the immune organs to shrink or to become atrophy.

(5) It was also found through experiments that some of the experimental mice did not have a successful vaccination or the tumor grew very small, and the thymus did not shrink significantly.

In order to understand the relationship between tumor and thymus atrophy, a group of experimental mice were excised when they transplanted solid cancer to the size of the thumb. 1 month after dissection, the thymus did not undergo progressive atrophy.

Therefore, it is speculated that a solid tumor may produce a factor that is not yet known to inhibit the thymus, which is temporarily called "cancer Thymus inhibition factor", pending further experimental research.

(6) The above experimental results prove that the progression of the tumor will cause progressive atrophy of the thymus. So can there be some ways to stop the host's thymus atrophy? Therefore, we began to use immune organ cell transplantation to restore the experimental function of immune organs. In the study of suppressing tumor progression, the thymus atrophy of the immune organs, looking for ways to restore the function of the thymus and reconstitute the immune system, using mice as the animals. The experimental study on the immune function of fetal liver, fetal spleen and fetal thymocyte transplantation was performed.

The results showed that S, T, L tertiary cells were transplanted together, and the tumor regression rate was 40% in the near future. The long-term tumor complete regression rate was for 46.67%, the tumor completely disappeared and long-term survival.

(7) When investigating the effect of tumor on the spleen of the immune organs of the body, it was found that the spleen had an inhibitory effect on tumor growth in the early stage of tumor. In the late stage of the tumor, the spleen also showed progressive atrophy. The experimental results suggest that The effect of spleen on tumor growth is bidirectional, with some inhibition in the early stage and no inhibition in the late stage. Spleen cell transplantation can enhance the inhibition of tumors.

(8) The results of follow-up suggest that controlled metastasis is the key to cancer treatment. There are many steps and links in the current known cancer cell transfer. In order to prevent one of the links to prevent its transfer, in 1986, the author's laboratory carried out microcirculation research work. Microcirculation microscopy was used to observe the microvascular formation and flow rate and flow rate of tumor-bearing mice.

(9) We design drugs for anti-tumor angiogenesis from natural medicines.

The Olympus microcirculation photomicrography system was used to observe the neovascularization process and count the flow rate and flow rate of the arterioles and venules. The TG, an extract of ethyl acetate, was found in Chinese herbal medicine to inhibit the formation of blood vessels. It was found that there was no neovascularization on the first day of inoculation, and microscopic neovascularization was observed on the second day, and TG could cause tumors. The neonatal microvessel density is reduced.

(10) From a large number of tumor-bearing animal models in the laboratory, it was also found that the experimental tumors inoculated subcutaneously in some tumor-bearing mice grew larger. The central tissue structure of the transplanted solid tumor is different from the surrounding cancer cells, and the center of the nodule is mostly sterile necrosis or liquefaction. The surrounding area is still active

4

cancer cells. Therefore, in the clinical treatment work, measures for treating sterile necrosis can be employed.

According to the results of laboratory experiments, it was found that resection of the thymus can produce a model of cancer-bearing animals, and it is found that the thymus is progressively atrophied during cancer. It is found that immunity is related to the occurrence and development of cancer, and low immunity is related to the metastasis of cancer.

The purpose of determining the next study and treatment is to:

1. to prevent thymus atrophy, increase thymus weight, increase immunity, that is, the principle of treatment of breast enhancement and preservation of blood.
2. Based on the above experimental findings, data and data, the experimental basis and theoretical basis of new concepts and methods for anticancer and anti-metastasis treatment were established, namely, preventing progressive atrophy of the thymus, protecting the thymus, increasing the weight of the thymus, increasing immunity, and protecting the bone marrow. Promote bone marrow stem cells and immunogenic cells to improve immune surveillance.
3. Established a new concept and new method, the principle, direction, experimental basis and theoretical basis of treatment, namely biological immunotherapy or XZ-C immunomodulation therapy.

How can I stop the thymus from shrinking and protect the thymus?

After 3 years of basic laboratory research in the laboratory, it was found that the thymus was progressively atrophied during cancer;

Cancer cells are made into animal models of cancer, and immunosuppression is related to the occurrence, development and metastasis of tumors. According to the experimental materials and data, it is determined that the treatment goal is to protect the thymus, increase the weight of the thymus, prevent the thymus atrophy, increase immunity, protect the Thymus and increasing immune function, protect the marrow and increase blood production, and establish the theoretical system of a new concept and new method for anticancer and anti-metastasis treatment and the theoretical basis of clinical practice.

What kind of method can prevent the thymus from shrinking and protect the thymus? The author found through experiments that the fetal chest and the fetus of the same kind of fetus were taken. With Liver and fetal spleen stem cell transplantation, the tumor disappearance rate reached 46.7% and had the good effects. However, these experimental results were difficult to use in clinical practice because human homologous fetal cells cannot be obtained. So it began to look for drugs that prevent thymus atrophy and protect the thymus from natural medicines.

(3) Experimental research on finding new anticancer and anti-metastatic drugs in natural medications

The experimental methods which search the new anti-cancer and anti-metastatic drugs from natural medicines.

1. In vitro screening experiment

    The cancer cells were cultured in vitro to observe the direct damage of the drug to the cancer cells, and the inhibition rate of cell proliferation caused by cytotoxicity was measured.

2. Inhibition of tumor in tumor-bearing animals

    Each batch of experiments consisted of 240 Kunming mice, divided into 8 groups, 30 in each group. The first to sixth groups were experimental groups. Each group was screened for 1 Chinese herbal medicine, the seventh group was blank control group, and the eighth group was treated with fluorouracil or cyclophosphamide which was used as the control group. The whole group of mice received the EAC or S-180 or H22 cancer cells 1×107/ ml in the right anterior sacral epithelium. After inoculation for 24 hours, each mouse was orally fed with crude bio-powder, weighing 1000 mg/kg, 1/d feeding for 4 weeks, observe survival, adverse reactions, calculate prolonged survival, calculate tumor inhibition rate.

    Among the 200 kinds of crude drugs, 48 of them have certain or even good tumor inhibition rates, and the inhibition rate on cancer cells is

    70% to 90% or more, the other 152 Chinese medicines have no inhibition rate for cancer.

The optimized combination was carried out to test the tumor inhibition rate in a tumor-bearing animal model to form XZ-C1-XZ-C10. Immunomodulatory granules, XZ-C1 can significantly inhibit cancer cells, but does not affect normal cells, XZ-C4 can protect Thymus and improve immune function, XZ-C8 can protect the marrow and produce blood, improve the quality of life, improve appetite, enhance physical fitness, Extend survival.

(4) clinical verification work

1. After 7 years of scientific experiments in the laboratory screening from natural medicines, XZ-C immunomodulated anti-cancer, anti-metastasis Chinese medications with Thymus enhancement and bone marrow protection and production of blood and activation of blood circulation and reduction of blood stasis were composed; on the basis of the success of animal experiments, clinical validation work have done.
2. Since 1985, he has carried out experiments on tumor-bearing mice in tumor-bearing mice, and has proven clinical efficacy in outpatient clinics.

However, there are few patients, and there is no medical record in the outpatient clinic (the medical records are all issued to the patients), and it is impossible to accumulate scientific research materials. It must walk the road with the big cooperation of scientific research.

3. Set up an anti-cancer research collaboration group, take the road of scientific research and cooperation, and jointly set up the road of tackling the difficulties, and set up the Shuguang Oncology Clinic.

4. Restore the outpatient medical record, fill in the complete and detailed outpatient medical record, and obtain the complete information of clinical verification, which is convenient for analysis and statistics, and is conducive to outpatient clinical research to improve the quality of medical care. It is conducive to outpatient clinical research to improve the quality of medical care.

5. The outpatient cases were kept and were followed up regularly. The experience and lessons of the diagnosis and treatment of this case were analyzed briefly for long-term observation of the treatment effectiveness.

6. The oncology clinic outpatient medical records are designed in a tabular format, which contains all relevant medical information and relevant epidemiological data, so as to facilitate Statistical analysis of its possible pathogenesis factors.

7. Review more than 1 year of cases, outpatient medical records, write a summary of medical records, and adding into the analysis of the large table. The large table contains each item or the content of the medical record form which are concise and detailed, and the Twilight Oncology Clinic has been verified for 34 years and more than 12,000 outpatient clinical data were collected for outpatient clinical research.

8. From experimental research to clinical research, from clinical to experimental, the collaborative group has experimental research bases and clinical application verification bases. The former is in the medical laboratory, the latter in the Twilight Oncology Clinic, from the experimental to the clinical, that is, based on the success of the experimental research, it has the clinical application; the new problems are discovered in the clinical application process, and further basic experimental research is carried out, and the new experimental results are used in clinical validation, such as outpatients with liver cancer with portal vein tumor thrombus, renal cancer patients with inferior vena cava tumor thrombus, some of which there are CT report and some of which are the pathological sections of the surgically removed specimens. In fact, the cancerous plug is the cancer cell group on the way to the metastasis. It is the third manifestation of cancer in the human body. When we discovered the tumor thrombosis problem, we began to conduct experimental research on the formation of cancerous thrombosis. Looking for new ways to fight against cancerous plugs and dissolve cancerous plugs, we found four kinds of traditional Chinese medicines that help to dissolve cancerous plugs, and found out the effective ingredients.

Such the experiment to clinical and repeated experiments to repeated clinical, continuous cycle of rising, after 12 years of clinical practice experience, the awareness continues to rise and to increase, summarizes the practice, analyzes and reflects, and the evaluation rises to the theory, and proposes new understanding, new thinking, and new treatment ideas.

9. 12 years of analysis, evaluation and reflection after a large number of outpatient consultations, a series of clinical problems were discovered and further research and improvement are needed.

10. Retrospective analysis and reflection from a large number of outpatient medical records, recognizing that many patients with postoperative adjuvant chemotherapy failed to prevent recurrence, and even promoted into immune failure, indicating that chemotherapy needs further research and improvement.

11. From the review, analysis and reflection of a large number of outpatient medical records, it is recognized that many patients have recurrence and metastasis soon after surgery. The design of "radical surgery treatment procedure" needs further research and improvement, how to do the intraoperative tumor-free technology, prevent and treat intraoperative cancer cells shedding and planting of cancer cells in the chest cavity or in the abdominal cavity or surgical field which are important measures to prevent postoperative recurrence and metastasis.

12. Through the collaborative group of focusing on a large number of cases of treatment practice, evaluation, analysis, reflection, it is experienced as the following points:

    (1) Current postoperative adjuvant chemotherapy on many patients fail to prevent cancer recurrence and metastasis.

    (2) The focus of anti-cancer should be anti-metastasis and recurrence, which is the key to improve the long-term efficacy of postoperative patients.

    (3) The "threshold" of anti-cancer should be "three early".

    (4) Anti-cancer recurrence must start from the surgery; from the data of outpatients, some radical surgery in the primary hospitals are not standardized, so the recurrence is early and the abdominal cavity is widely metastasized. It is advisable to strengthen the standardized and standardized education and learning of cancer surgery.

    (5) Some patients with postoperative cancer have weak body strengthen or constitution, and they are all 4 cycles of chemotherapy or 6 cycles of chemotherapy, which promotes immune function decline or even failure. Why should the 4 cycles or 6 cycles be, what is the theoretical basis or experimental data? From the domestic and foreign literature, there is no theoretical basis for laboratory experiments of 4 courses of chemotherapy or 6 courses of treatment in the literature.

13. Through 14 years of contact with a large number of outpatients, review, analysis, reflection, evaluation, the current diagnosis of cancer mainly relies on pathological

slides, but pathological sections must be obtained after surgery, intraoperative or endoscopic biopsy or puncture, which is in the middle and late stages, so that it must try to study new methods for early diagnosis and new tumor markers.

14. From the time of the positive performance on CT, MRI, and color Doppler examinations of a large number of outpatients, cancer was found by CT, MRI, and color ultrasound. Most patients are in the advanced stage, and some have lost the opportunity for surgery. Therefore, we should try to find new technologies, new markers and new diagnostic methods that can be used as the early stages.

15. Clinical efficacy observation: Based on experimental research, it has been applied to various types of cancer since 1994, mostly patients were in stage III or IV, that is, advanced cancer that cannot be removed by exploration; those with recent or long-term metastasis or recurrence after various cancer operations; Liver metastases, lung metastases, brain metastases, bone metastases, or cancerous pleural effusions, cancerous ascites, all kinds of cancer palliative resection, exploration can only do gastrointestinal anastomosis or colostomy and cancer can not be removed; patients should not be surgery, radiotherapy, chemotherapy and so on. XZ-C immunomodulation anticancer Chinese medicine has been clinically applied for 14 years, and systematic observation has achieved obvious curative effect. No adverse reactions were observed after long-term use. Clinical observations have shown that XZ-C immunomodulatory Chinese medicine can comprehensively improve the quality of life of patients with advanced cancer and improve immunity and control cancer cell proliferation, consolidate and enhance long-term efficacy after surgery or radiotherapy.

16. Oral and external application XZ-C medicine has good curative effect on softening and reducing surface metastasis of tumor, combined with intervention or intubation pump treatment. It can protect the liver, kidney, bone marrow hematopoietic system and immune organs and improve immunity. In the Department of Twilight Oncology Clinic, 4698 cases of stage III, IV or metastatic recurrent cancer were treated for long-term follow-up or follow-up.

17. The evaluation of quality of life in patients with advanced cancer of taking XZ-C immunomodulation Chinese medicine:

this group are middle and advanced patients, after taking the drug, the improvement rate was 93.2%, the spirit improved by 95.2%, the appetite improved by 93%, and the physical strength increased by 57.3%, which improved the quality of life of patients with advanced cancer.

The 42nd Annual Meeting of the American Society of Clinical Oncology (ASCO) proposed that comprehensive assessment of patients' quality of life is one of the main treatment goals. A total of 223 articles in the 2006 (ASCO) conference paper were related to the quality of life of patients, accounting for 5.8% of the total number of papers. Quality of life has become an important factor that people must consider when choosing a treatment strategy. The understanding of the purpose of anti-tumor treatment has made people more and more improve the quality of life of cancer patients as one of the main purposes of treatment. A large number of studies have begun to take the impact of treatment on quality of life as the main evaluation index.

18. XZ-C anti-cancer analgesic effect:

Pain is a more obvious and painful symptom in patients with advanced cancer, just like analgesics for cancerous pain, the pain has no great effect, the anesthetic analgesic has addiction and analgesic effect. XZ-C anti-analgesic analgesic has strong analgesic effect and long maintenance time. After 298 cases, the effective rate is 78.0%. The total effective rate is 95.3%. There is no obvious adverse reaction, no addiction, and stable analgesic effect. It is an effective treatment for cancer patients to relieve pain and improve their quality of life.

19. Efficacy evaluation:

It not only pays attention to the short-term efficacy and imaging indicators, but also pays more attention to the long-term efficacy of survival, quality of life and immune indicators. The goal is to have patients with long time and good quality of life.

Pay attention to changes in symptoms and improvement of symptoms during medication; it is valid for lasting more than 1 month, otherwise it is invalid. It is effective to pay attention to the spirit, good appetite, and quality of life (Carson's score) for more than 1 month, otherwise it will be invalid. The evaluation criteria for solid tumor mass were classified into 4 grades according to the size of the tumor, that is, the grade 1 mass disappeared, the grade II mass was reduced by 1/2, the grade III mass became soft, and the grade IV mass did not change or increase.

B. The Summary of our product information

XZ-C immunomodulatory anticancer medications are the selected 48 kinds of anti-tumor Chinese herbal medications with the better cancer inhibitory rate from traditional Chinese herbal medications in the tumor-bearing mice experiments. After made up into the composition of the compound, and then tested in the inhibiting tumor experiments in cancer-bearing mice, the compound inhibitory rate is much greater than single herb. $XZ-C_1$, $XZ-C_4$ are consisted of 28 Chinese herbal medications, of which $XZ-C_{1-A}$, $XZ-C_{1-B}$ can 100% inhibit cancer and 100% don't kill normal cells with righting and firming the body, improve the role of the body's immune function. From our experiments XZ-C pharmacodynamic study the results show: they has a good inhibitory rate on **Ehrlich ascites carcinoma, S_{182}, H_{22} hepatocellular carcinoma**; there are obvious synergy and toxicity attenuation; the experiments also demonstrated that XZ-C immune regulation and control traditional Chinese medications have significantly improved immune function.

After the acute toxicity test in mice, there is no obvious toxicity and no significant side effects for the long-term oral clinical taking (2--6 years). XZ-C can significantly reduce the toxicity of chemotherapy while the oral immune regulation medications are used with chemotherapy. The oral XZ-C drugs can increase the white blood cells; the hemoglobin increases during the Chemotherapy Intermittent periods. The advanced cancer patients mostly have weakness, fatigue, loss of appetite. After taking XZ-C immunomodulatory anticancer medications 4-8-12 weeks, the patients have more significantly improved on the appetite and sleeping and have the relieved pain and gradually recuperate.

2

We have been carried out experimental studies and clinical validation work

A. Experimental Research Work

In our laboratory conducted the following experiment study new cancer screening from traditional Chinese medication and anti-metastatic drug:

1. an in vitro screening test:

    the use of cancer cells in vitro, we observed cancer drugs directly to cancer cells damage. Cultured cancer cells in a test tube, were placed raw meal drug products (500ug / mI) to observe whether there is inhibition and inhibition rate of cancer cells.

2. Screening test of tumor-inhibition in vivo:

    Manufacture cancer-bearing animal model for the screening of Chinese herbs for cancer-bearing animal experiments suppressor rate, batch experiments with mice 24. They were divided into eight experimental groups, each group 3. Only the first group was the control group 7, Group 8 with a 5-F. Or CTX control group. The whole group of mice were inoculated with EAC or 518. Or H22 cancer cells inoculated after 24h, each rat oral feeding crude product of crude drug powder, long screened Adams fed the herb, observed survival inhibition rate was calculated.

    As this, we conducted experimental study for four consecutive years, and each year 100. Multiple tumor-bearing animal model years made a total of nearly 6,000 tumor-bearing animal models, each bought were carried out after the test mice died of liver, spleen, sheets, pituitary gland, kidney pathological anatomy, a total of 20,000 times slices.

3. Experimental results:

    In our laboratory animal experiments after screening 200 kinds of Chinese herbal medicine, the screening must know certainly has some, even excellent inhibitory effect

12

on cancer cells, inhibition rate of more than 75-90%. The note by animal experiments screened-out to 152 kinds of no significant anti-cancer effect.

B. Clinical validation

Based on animal experiments successfully, clinical validation was tested:

1. Methods:

Oncology clinics and combination anti-cancer, anti-metastasis, relapse research collaboration group, keep medical records, establish and improve the follow-up observation system to observe long-term effects. From experimental study to clinical verification. new problems are found during the clinical application, which need fundamental experimental studies. Afterwards new experimental results are applied to clinical verification. Experiments → clinic → experiments once more → clinic once more, recurrent ascent continuously; through eight-year clinical practical experiences, knowledge also continues to improve. Summation, analysis, reflection and evaluation ascend to theory, putting forward new knowledge, new concept, new thought, new strategy and new therapeutic route and scheme.

Clinical criteria are: good quality of life, longer survival

Results: XZ-C immunomodulatory anticancer medicine was observed in many advanced cancer patients and found that the results was significant.

2. Clinical information

China Anti-cancer Research Cooperation of Chinese Traditional Medicine and Western Medicine, Anti Carcinoma Metastasis and Recurrence Research Office and Shuguang Tumor Specialized Outpatient Department had treated 4, 698 carcinoma patients with Stage III and IV or in metastasis and recurrence who were treated with Z-C medications of immune regulation and control combined with western medicine and chinese from 1994 to Nov. 2002, among which there were 3, 051 men patients and 1,647 women patients. The youngest one was 11 years old and the oldest one was 86 years oldt. All groups of the patients were entirely subject to the diagnosis of pathological histology or definitive diagnosis with ultrasonic B, CT and MRI iconography. According to the staging standard of UICC, all the cases were entirely the patients in medium and advanced stage over Stage III. In this group, there were 1,021 hepatic carcinoma patients; there were 752 patients suffering from carcinoma of lung; there were 694 gastric carcinoma patients, 624 patients suffering from esophagus cardia carcinoma, 328 patients suffering from rectum carcinoma of anal canal, 442 patients suffering from carcinoma of colon, 368 patients suffering from breast carcinoma, 74 patients suffering from adenocarcinoma of pancreas, 30 patients suffering from carcinoma of bile duct, 43 patients suffering from retroperitoneal tumor, 38 patients suffering from oophoroma, 9 patients suffering from cervical carcinoma, 11 patients suffering from cerebroma, 34 patients suffering from thyroid carcinoma, 38 patients suffering from nasopharyngeal carcinoma, 9 patients suffering from melanoma, 27 patients suffering from kidney carcinoma, 48 patients suffering from carcinoma of urinary bladder, 13 patients suffering from leukemia, 47 patients suffering from metastasis of supraclavicular lymph nodes, 35 patients suffering various fleshy tumors and 39 patients suffering from other malignancies.

3. Drugs and administration methods:

The principle of cancer treatment is to protect Thymus and to increase immune function and to protect bone marrow and to produce more blood, so as to enhance the host's immune surveillance and to control the cancer escape. From the Chinese medicine aspects, the principle of treatment is to support the rightness and to remove the evil and to soft the hardness and to reduce the nodule and to supply the gas and blood both, which the drugs are the following : XZ-C1, XZ-C2, XZ a C3, XZ-C4, XZ-C5, XZ-C6, XZ-C7, XZ-C8.........., XZ-C10, depending on the different cancer, illness, metastasis case and according to the disease dialectical. The selection of these drugs would be made. Metastatic cancer or solid tumor mass, both oral anti-cancer medications and topical anti-cancer cream or ointment; if there is cancer pain in the patient, the topical analgesic cream would be used; for the patients with jaundice and ascites, the soup with eliminating the jaundice or the soup with reducing the water would be used.

4. Treatment Results:

Symptoms had the improvement; the qualityof life are improvement and the survival terms are prolonged.

(1) Among the 4,277 carcinoma patients in medium and advanced stage who took Z-C medicine with the return visit over 3 months, the case history had the specific observation record of the curative effect, see Table 1.

Table 1 4277 cases of efficacy observation to improve overall quality of life in patients with advanced cancer

Improve ment	Spirit	Appetite	Physical strength	Enhance general situation	Wight increase	Sleep improve ment	Improve activities and capacity restricted relief	Self-care Walking activity	Resume work as usual and Engaged in light body
Cases	4071	3986	2450	479	2938	1005	1038	3220	479
(%)	95.2	93.2	57.3	11.2	68.7	23.5	24.3	75.3	11.2

In this group, all of them were the patients in medium and advanced stage. After taking the medicine, their symptoms were improved to different extents with the effective rate of 93.2%. With respect to the improvement of the quality of life (as per Karnofsky Performance Status), it rose to 80 scores on average after administration from 50 on average before administration; the patients in this group met with the different metastasis and dysfunction of the organs about Stage III. It was reported by the previous statistic information that the mesoposition survival time of this kind of patients was about 6 months. The longest time among this group of the cases reached up to 18 years; in the rest of the cases the average survival time reached more than one year; one case of primary liver cancer on the left lobe had the right lobe recurrence after removing the life lobe cancer, at that time XZ-C medication was taken only and the patient has been living more than 18 years now; another patient suffering from hepatic carcinoma had taken Z-C medicine for ten years and a half; two patients suffering from hepatic carcinoma met with frequency encountered carcinomatous lesion in the left and right liver and it entirely subsided through secondary CT reexamination after the patient took Z-C medicine for half a year and the state of the disease had been stable over half a year. One patient suffering from double-kidney carcinoma met with the widespread metastasis of abdominal cavity after removal of one kidney, after taking Z-C medicine, he was entirely recovered and began to work again. 3 patients suffering from carcinoma of lung, with the lung not removed through exploration, had taken Z-C medicine over three years and a half. 2 patients suffering from gastric remnant carcinoma had taken XZ-C medicine for 8 years. 3 patients suffering from reoccurrence of rectal carcinoma had taken XZ-C medicine for 3 years. 1 patient suffering from metastatic liver and rib of the mastocarcinoma had taken XZ-C medicine for 8 years. 1 patient suffering from the recurrent bladder carcinoma after operation of renal carcinoma had not met with the carcinoma for 9 years and a half after taking XZ-C medicine. All of these patients were the ones in the medium and advanced stage that could not be operated once more or treated with radiotherapy or chemotherapy. They only took XZ-C medicine without other medicines for treatment. Up to today, they are reexamined and get the medicine at the out-patient department every month. **Through taking the medicine for a long time, the state of the disease is controlled in the stable state to make the organism and the tumor in balanced state for a relatively long time and get a relatively good survival with tumor, in this way, the symptoms of the patients are improved, the quality of life is improved and the survival time is prolonged.**

(2) As to 84 patients suffering from solid tumor and 56 patients suffering from enlargement of upper lymph node of metastatic compact bone, after taking Z-C series medicines orally and applying Z-C3 anti-cancer apocatastasis paste, they met with good curative effects, see table 2.

Table 2 Changes of 84 patients suffering from solid tumor and 56 patients suffering from metastatic mode after applying Z-C paste externally

	Solid tumor				Enlargement of upper lymph node of metastatic compact bone			
	Disappearance	Shrinkage 1/2	Softening	No change	Disappearance	Shrinkage 1/2	Softening	No change
No. of cases	12	28	32	12	12	22	14	8
(%)	14.2	33.3	38.0	14.2	21.4	39.2	25.0	14.2
Total effective rate (%)	85.7				85.7			

(3) 298 patients suffering from carcinoma pain obtained the obvious pain alleviation effects after taking Z-C medicine orally and applying Z-C anti-cancer apocatastasis paste externally, see Table 3.

Clinical menifetation	Pain			
	Light alleviation	Obvious alleviation	Disappearance	Avoidance
No of cases	52	139	93	14
(%)	17.3	46.8	31.2	4.7
Total effective rate (%)	95.3			

3

Immune pharmacology of XZ-C immune regulation and control medication

Compared the traditional Chinese medication pharmacology with western medication immunity pharmacology, each has own characteristics and advantages which the long-term clinical experience of Chinese medication has accumulated a large number of prescriptions regulating body's immune function, especially the beneficial Chinese medications generally have dynamic regulation of the immune benefits.

Whether the single herb medication or prescription will have a variety of active ingredients, and unlike the western medication (synthetic drugs) it is a matter of a single structure. The roles of Chinese medications have many aspects, in addition to the regulation of immune function, which has a certain role on the whole system function.

The main role of XZ-C immune regulation and control medications regulates the cellular immune response which regulate all of the cell-mediated, including various cytokines or lymphokines. The immune function of XZ-C medication has the major role on stem cells immunity, such as the thymus, gonads and lymphatic systems and T, B cells and various cytokines.

China ancient medication has the concept of that righteousness isn't weak or false and evil doesn't come into which constitutes an integral part of traditional Chinese medication theory. **Its essence is to maintain the balance of the overall function and to enhance resistance to disease**. Its main role is to enhance the host immune function, in fact, the tonics medication is based on immune pharmacology. Immunity pharmacology is an emerging interdisciplinary and serves as a bridge contact between pharmacology and immunology. XZ-C immune control regulation medication has obvious immune promoting function, as an effective immune enhancers, this area should be vigorously developed to get a new type of immune accelerator, making them become reliable, efficient and safe drugs. The various Chinese herbs in XZ-C4 have substantially immune enhancer effects. In animal experiments XZ-C4 have been proven to significantly promote thymus function. The main role of Chinese medication immunomodulator is to regulate cellular immune and various cell-mediated immune response, including cytokines or lymphokines.

4

The pharmacological research of XZ-C immune regulation and control anticancer Chinese medications

1. To sum anticancer pharmacology and experimental cancer-bearing animal solid tumors in vivo anti-tumor experiments, XZ-C drugs have significant anti-tumor effects. The inhibition rate of antitumor activity $XZ-C_1$ medication among XZ-C medications was 58% in the first six weeks; the inhibition rate of XZ-C4 was 70% in the first six weeks; the inhibition rate of cyclophosphamide amine (CTX) was 49% in the first 6 weeks in liver cancer H_{22} bearing mice. Life span in $XZ-C_1$ was 9.8% which indicates XZ-C drug has a good anti-cancer effect.

2. XZ-C drug has synergistic effect of attenuating the toxicity from chemotherapy drugs, as said anti-cancer pharmacology above, XZ-C4 has been shown to have better function to reduce the toxicity from chemotherapy.

3. XZ-C anti-cancer medication protects immune hematopoietic function. Chemotherapy drugs such as MMC or CTX cause bone marrow hematopoietic system suppression such as WBC↓, PLT↓, and then treated by or served by XZ-C4 for 4 weeks, Hb, WBC, PLT were improved significantly in cancer-bearing mice.

4. XZ-C immunomodulatory anticancer medication has a role in protecting the immune organs and improving human immune function.

In the above H22 tumor-bearing mice, after CTX was taken, it caused leukopenia, reduced immune function and kidney damaged on pathologic slices ; after taking XZ-C4, it can significantly improve immune function and can recover white blood cells and red blood cells in H_{22} cancer-bearing mice. There is no thymic atrophy but a little hypertrophy, lymphocytes intensive, increased epithelial reticular cells in XZ-C treatment group.

5

The research on cytokine induction factors of XZ-C anticancer immune regulation and control medication

1. XZ-C4 induces endogenous cytokines

    (1) Through the experiments: XZ-C4 has many immune strengthening functions and has closely relationship to the induced endogenous cytokines
    (2) XZ-C4 can recover the reduction of the white blood cells, granulation cells and platelets.
    (3) XZ-C4 can have the direct function on GM-CSF production from granulation cell (GM) through IL-1β, also increase TNF, IFN etc all of kind of the cell factors, which are possible the indirect function.
    (4) XZ-C4 can increase the Th1 cell factors, which were decrease in the cancer patients. There are the curative effects on the anemia and the white blood cells decrease due to the chemotherapy.
    (5) The experiment analysis showed that XZ-C4 not only protects the bone marrow function, but also has direct function on the tumor cell division through cytokines.

In brief, XZ-C4 can induce the tumor division and natural death through **the autocrine** which produce all of kind of factors. The autocrine is the secretory things from the host to affect the host's function. XZ-C4 probably will become the induction therapy to the tumor division in the future.

2. XZ-C4 inhibiting cancer development and metastasis

The malignant development is defined as tumor cells accepting invasion and metastasis characters during the proliferation. To research Cancer development needs to have good repeated animal models. Then the good repeated animal model was made from the mice fibrosis cancernoma QR-32. QR-32 cannot proliferate after inoculation in the skin, and will completely disappear; there were no metastasis lump after injecting into the vein. However, if QR-32 was injected with Gelatin sponge together under the skin in the mice, QR-32 will become the proliferating tumor cells QRSP.XuZe XuJie Bin Wu• 140 •

19

In vitro culturing QRSP and then transfer into another mice, even if there is no foreign thing, the tumors will grow such as the lung metastasis will happen after injection in the vein.

XZ-C4 was used in the animal models to search the effects of the tumor development. To divide this animal models into two steps: the process from QR-32 to QRSP(early progress) and from the QRSP to tumor(later progress). After using XZ-C4, the tumor development will be inhibited in these two models, especially the former will be inhibited significantly. And this has relationship with the dose of the medication.

On the survival experiment the animal models of the inoculation of the QR-32 AND Gelatin sponge died during 65 days, however in XZ-C group the mice survival rate for 150 days was 30%.

XZ-C4 can increase the immune effects and reduce the side effects of other anticancer medication in the previous experimental and clinical verification.

This research proved that XZ-C4 has inhibition of the cancer progression function and inhibit cancer invasion and metastasis.

6

The toxicology studies of XZ-C immunomodulatory anticancer medication

$XZ-C_1$ can be long-term use. Acute toxicity experiments showed that: 100 times the adult dose to mice fed (10g / kg) were observed at 24, 48, 72, 96 hours in 30 purebred mice without a death. The median lethal dose (LD50) is difficult to be measured out and is a quite secure prescription.

According to WHO "cancer medicine and acute toxin Classification Standard" assessment patients with different measurement, different forms of treatment, changes in the peripheral blood, liver and kidney function in order to understand its toxicity and adverse circumstances, XZ-C medication was oral taken in more than 6000 cases, continuous medication at less 3 months, some for years. The patients have no abnormal phenomenon before and after treatment and blood tests such as WBC, RBC, Hb, PLT are checked and the results are improvement. In order to control cancers the patients with advanced cancer in our specialty clinics took XZ-C for a long-term such as using $XZ-C_{1+}4$ 10 or more years and the patient didn't have metastasis and non-proliferation, the disease condition is stable, and lived with cancer. Adhere to long-term medication XZ-C medication can stabilize condition, inhibit cancer proliferation, improve the quality of life and prolong their lives, did not show toxicity, **we insist on a longer-term experience serving XZ-C medicine and can help prevent the patients from short and long term recurrence and metastasis after radical surgery.**

7

The active ingredient of XZ-C anticancer immune control and regulation medications

$XZ\text{-}C_{1+4}$ is a compound consisting of 28 Chinese herbs. The extraction work of total effective ingredient compound is extremely difficult, the technology is complex and it was exceedingly difficult to extract the active ingredient compound. Active ingredients of a single herb can be extracted. Thus, XZ- C series drugs except $XZ\text{-}C_1$ outside is boiling agent, and the rest are used every herb of fine powder or capsules in order to remain independent of each herb's active ingredients which can play its antitumor effects. The powders are mixed fine powder and the active ingredient can remain independent of each drug; however, after the drug is boiled, the chemical element changes so as to inevitably change the active ingredient of the drug and make it difficult to know the active ingredients after boiling.

But overall the active ingredients of various medications in the prescription are:

1. Alkaloids
2. Glycosides: saponins and glycosides

Each herb in the prescription has anti-tumor active ingredient, for example prescription Ganoderma lucidum, its anti-tumor component A is Ganoderma lucidum polysaccharides, antitumor effect is: with a hypodermic method, graft inoculation 7 days of S_{180} ascites carcinoma on mouse right groin, at a dose 20% mg / kg 10 days the inhibition rate is 95.6-98.5%. The inhibition rate of treatment of leukopenia was 84.6%, the treatment of leukopenia, recent efficiency 84.6% and total WBC increases 1028 / mm3. Anti-tumor component B is Fumaric acid. Its anti-tumor effect: with Gavage 60mg / kg 10 days in S180 cancer mice, then weighed tumors: the inhibition rate was 37.1% -38.6% and the body weight of mice did not decline.

Another example is the prescription Fructus ligustri lucidi, its anti-tumor components is ursolic acid. Its anti-tumor effect on liver cancer cells in vitro with a very significant inhibition rate, can prolong life Ehrlich ascites carcinoma in mice. Pharmacological experiments show its flooding agent capable of inhibiting certain animals transplanted tumor growth. This product contains oleanolic acid with enhancing immune function, recovering peripheral leukocyte, enhancing phagocytes in reticuloendothelial cells, recovers white blood cells of the reduction induced by radiation or chemotherapy, strengthens cardiac functions and diuretic function and protects liver function.

Another example is the prescription of Sophora, its anti-tumor component A: Sophocarpine. Its anti-tumor effect: In vitro experiments showed that Sophocarpine have a direct killing effect on Ehrlich ascites tumor cells: the inhibition rate was 30 to 60% on mice transplanted U_{14} or S_{180}. There is clinical application effect. Sophora antitumor component B is Oxymatrine. Its anti-tumor effects: for S_{180} mice there is significant activity, 500ug and 250 ug per day administration, a total of five days, in treatment groups, respectively tumor weight was 26.1% and 57.9%.

3. Another example is the prescription of bamboo ginseng, its anti-tumor component A, as β-Elemene. Its anti-tumor effects: on the EAC, ARS etc two kinds of ascites cancer there is significant anti-graft tumor effect; also it has effect on YAS and S180 ascites. Its anti-tumor components: ginseng total polysaccharides. Its anti-tumor effects of animal experiments show: total ginseng polysaccharides has a stimulating effect on immune function for Ehrlich ascites cancer in mice at 400- 800mg / kg with significant cancer inhibition. Ginseng polysaccharide on many tumor cells doesn't have directly killing effect and its anti-tumor effect may be due to the adjustment of the body's immune function so that cancer-bearing host enhanced antitumor capacity. Its anti-tumor component C is Ginsenoside which has inhibition for S180 cancer cells which its tumor weight inhibition rate was 36.4% in 120mg / kg 7d. Ginsenosides may act directly on cancer cells to inhibit cancer cell growth; also available through effects on metabolism and regulation of immunity so that the body's resistance to disease increased and tumor growth was inhibited. Ginseng extract can inhibit Marine tumor, sarcoma S_{180} and lung cancer T_{55}.

8

The Principles of XZ-C Prescription

XZ-C1,XZ-C4 of XZ-C immunomodulatory anticancer medications are compound as a powder, or capsules, the compound is a mixture rather than multi-flavored powder, so each herb's active ingredients, pharmacological effects are alone Each herb can be individually separated.

XZ-C compound is completely different with decocton in the traditional Chinese medicine. After A, B, C, D compound are boiled, the component is completely changed, like eating, "pot", the original pharmacological effect of every taste was widowed after boiling together, and the original pharmacological effect of each flavor was lost after boiled, and after cooking it is difficult to know what the pharmacological effects and what the active ingredient is. It is very difficult and very complex technology to extract the active ingredient after boiling the compound. Our XZ-C drugs are completely different, not boiling, every individual taste is grinded into fine level, and then mixed in different amounts (cannot afford a compound effect), the pharmacological effects of each herb and its active ingredient completely do not change while retaining all herbs and pharmacological effects of the active ingredient. **This is the reform and innovation for traditional Chinese medicine formulations.**

Why use compound rather than single herb? Because the role of power is not enough, more herbs together have stronger effects such as A = a + b + c + d. then there must be A> a, A> a + b, A> a + b + c, etc., such as the inhibition rate of its single flavor was 20%, another flavor was 30%, and then another 31%, which totally the inhibition rate of this mixed serving may be 20 + 30 + 31 which may reach 81%. To improve the immune system, such as one flavor is 19%, the second flavor is 40%, the third flavor is 24%, then the mixed one together may be 83%. Holding constant every individual taste is the most important; each herb play its independent role in anti-cancer and increasing the role of immunity function.

Furthermore, XZ-C prescription principles also are followed the biological characteristics of cancer and cancer metastasis multi-link, multi-step characteristics so over the years we achieved remarkable results on anti-recurrence and anti-metastasis for the patients with long-term XZ-C immunomodulatory medications. Many patients with advanced cancer are inoperable and also should not have radiation and chemotherapy; however after long-term taking XZ-C immune regulation medication can achieve stable condition, control metastasis, improve quality of life and significantly prolong survival time. Every herb in XZ-C immunomodulatory anticancer medication was selected by two step in solid tumor-bearing mice in vivo anti-tumor screening:

the first step is screening a single flavor for the better inhibition rate, and the second step is to select prescription which there are three indicators: 1). it has a good anti-tumor effect; 2).without damage the normal cells of the body 3).increase immune function. If it has a high inhibition rate, but reduced immunity, it will not be chosen. In "new concept and new methods of cancer treatment," recently published a book written specifically for 16 years in our laboratory experiments work in cancer research confirmed cancer development and recurrence, metastasis and host immune organ function and immunity have certainly clear relationship. The medication which protects the immune organs and enhances immunity function are more important than the medication which inhibit or kill cancer drugs. XZ-C anti-tumor immune regulation medicine through experimental research and clinical validation observations show that:

1. There is significant anti-tumor effect, a higher inhibition rate;
2. Better improve the body's immune function, it can be cancer mouse experiments showed incomplete atrophy of the thymus and improve immune function;
3. Protect the hematopoietic system of the role of the chemotherapy drugs inhibit the outer periphery of the bone marrow after the white blood cells, platelets, red blood cells have been significantly improved;
4. Have a good effect for advanced cancer patients. Can significantly change the patient's appetite, sleep, physical and mental state, can significantly improve symptoms, improve quality of life;
5. Have a role in reducing the toxicity in advanced cancer patients with chemotherapy drugs. Its efficacy is superior to the treatment of chemotherapy drugs;
6. In animal experiments there is no toxic side effects. In clinics for 34 years on 12000 patients with advanced cancer the medication were used for a long-term 3--5 years, and some patients even served 8--10 years, it showed no toxic side effects. If the patients have long-term medication adherence, their spirit, appetite, physical strength are good, significantly prolonged survival.

9

Anti-tumor components of XZ-C immunomodulation anti-cancer Chinese medications ; structural formula; existing parts; anti-tumor effect

(1)   Z-C1 - A ApL

Anti-tumor component: agrimonniin
Effective part: Whole grass for the plant.

Anti-tumor effect:

Okucla and other scholars isolated agrimonniin from ApL grass, which has been proved to be the main component of anti-cancer. Before and after inoculation of MM2 breast cancer cells, this product was given 10 mg/kg ip, and as a result, all tumors were excluded, and the survival of tumor-bearing animals was prolonged regardless of PO or ip administration. Agrimonnia inhibits the growth of MH134 liver cancer and Meth-A cellulose sarcoma. In the medium with or without calf serum, MM2 breast cancer cells and Agrimonnia were treated for 2 h, then cultured in a 37^0 C humidified $CO2$ incubator for 48 h, and it was found that when calf serum was not added. Agrimonniin has a strong cytotoxic effect on MM2 cells. Its IC_{50} is 2.66ug / ml, but the addition of bovine fetal serum to the medium, the effect is reduced to about 4%, that is, the IC_{50} is 6.25% ug / ml. After intraperitoneal injection of Agriminnia for 4 days, MM2 breast cancer, MH134 liver cancer cells H3-thymidine nuclear uptake rate was significantly inhibited. Or Before and after inoculation of MM2 breast cancer cells, this product was given 10 mg/kg ip,the results were all tumor are rejected. No matter how it was given by P.O. or I.P., it can prolong survival time in tumor-bearing animals. Agrimonniin can inhibit MH 134 liver cancer and sarcoma Meth-A cellulose growth. With or without calf serum medium, MM2 breast cancer cells and agrimonniin together for 2h, then for 48h at 37 humidified $CO2$ incubator, and found time without calf serum, agrimonnii on breast cancer cells showed MM2 strong cytotoxicity, and its IC_{50} is 2.66ug / ml, but adding fetal calf serum in the culture medium, then weakened to around 4% of the original, namely an IC_{50} of 62.5% ug / ml, after intraperitoneal injection of agrimonniin 4d, the absorption of H^3- thymine on MM2 breast cancer and MH134 hepatoma cells was obviously inhibited.

These results indicate that agrimonniin is a potent anti-tumor acid and its anti-tumor effect may be due to the drug action on tumor cells and enhance the immune re ApL grass produces 1: 1, PH6.5 (1g crude drug / ml) solution by water extraction method to inhibit $_{S180,}$ cervix U_{14}, brain tumors B_{22}, Ehrlich EAC, melanoma B_{10}, rats W_{256} cancer. The results show that for more than transplanted tumors better inhibition, the inhibition rates were between 36.2 -6.59%, P<0.05, there is a significant difference.

ApL grass water extract has a strong inhibitory effect on human JTC-26 canein vitro and inhibition rate reaches 100% and meanwhile it promotes the growth 100%. While 30mg / kg ApL grass phenol was injected daily in intraperitoneal cavity, it has a significant therapeutic effect on rat sarcoma S_{37} and cervical cancer U_{14}. The inhibition rates on tumor growth were 47.0% and 38.7%. The inhibition was 47.4% on sarcoma S_{180} mice with 0.625g / day and was 52.6% on liver cancer.

Fluid extracted from liver cancer ascites was diluted with sterile physiological water 1-2x10⁷/ ml, then inoculated into mice, each mouse by intraperitoneal injection 0.2ml, the next day were randomly divided into treatment group and control group 30mg / ApL grass phenol was injected in intraperitoneal cavity once daily for 7 days, saline was injected in control group, then observed 30 days to calculate life span. Results: the mean survival day was 26.2 disabilities 0.9 in 24 animals treatment group; the average rival was 17.5 + 1.3day in control group. Life span prolonged above 49.6%. ApL grass phenol has significantly prolong life in animal liver cancer ascites carcinoma.

(2)　Z-C_1 - B SLT

Anti-tumor components: p-SoIamarine
Structure:

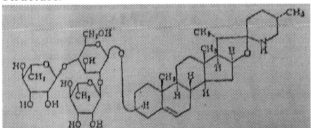

Effective parts: the SLT whole plant.

Anti-tumor effect: the whole plant has anti-tumor effect, in many countries for a long time as a folk medicine to cure cancer, p-Solamarine its active ingredient, at 30mg / kg on S_{180} mice the tumor weight from control group 1285 mg reduced to 274mg, the Inhibition rate was 78.6%.

The whole plant has anti-cancer effects on human lung cancer.

The studies have reported recently, extracted from the SLT anti-tumor active ingredient o health foods, it has given anti-tumor effect and almost no toxicity. SLT also contain solanine Australia which has inhibitory activity on S_{180} mice.

Recently it has been reported: an effective anti-tumor ingredient was extracted from SLT through water or an organic solvent or a mixture of water capacitive solvent, then be made into oral or parenteral medication: the oral dose serving as 1g /d; the parenteral drug as 60mg / d. The drug can inhibit a variety of tumors, such as S_{180} neck cancer with its low toxicity. Murakami Kotaro etc isolated two different body sugar from SLT, each with some anti-tumor effect.

SIT can inhibit S_{180}, cervical cancer U_{14} and Ehrlich ascites carcinoma. In vitro the product of hot water extract can has inhibition rate 100% on human cervical cancer JTC-26 system. And there was no effect on normal cells; in vivo experiments on mice S_{180} inhibition rate was 14.57%. This product contains an effective anti-cancer ingredient β-bitter solanine which significantly inhibited mice S_{180} and W256 mouse cancer.

(3)   Z-C_1-C SNL

Antitumor Ingredient A: Vitamin A
Structure:

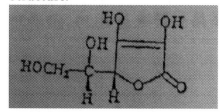

Existing parts: the whole plant for an amount of 9666 IU%.

Anti-tumor effects: vitamin A(Va) has anti-tumor activity. Wald had conducted a survey in 1975-1979, indicating Va having anti-tumor effect in vivo; Bontwell found that Va can stop cell membrane mucopolysaccharides aggregate effect induced by tumor promoters and block the receptor which bindstumor promoters. A new method for cancer treatment: normal sugar plus LETS (large cells are transferred outside sensitive protein from), two of which are affected Va material synthesis, which shows Va is important in cancer treatment. Meanwhile, Va and their derivatives can reverse cancerous cells inducedv by chemical carcinogens, viruses, and ionizing radiation.

Antitumor Component B: Vitamin C(Vc)
Structure:

Existing parts: the whole plant for the plant, its content is 20mg%

Anti-tumor effects: Vc is antioxidants in anti-tumor effects in blocking nitrite and primary amine to synthesize carcinogenicity compounds in vivo. Cameron will use 10g / day Vc to hundred cancer patients from long-term, 42 times of higher efficacy than control group and has better effect in gastrointestinal cancer. Murata use Vc high-dose to treat cervical cancer and its effect is 5.7 times higher than the effect of small doses. Malistratos induced sarcoma growth with benzo, then treat them with lots of Vc. Vc inhibited sarcoma growth and occurrence. For bladder cancer and skin cancer, it has the preventive effect. In epidemiology cancer occurrence is also related with the intake of Vc.

Vc with various anticancer drugs in combination can increase the efficacy of the drug. As with Vincristine (VCR) it has a synergistic effect and V + CCNu have higher treatment efficacy than single CCNu in leukemia. The survival time extencle: twice, but also alleviate the condition of patients with advanced cancer. Cisplatin anticancer drugs, because of its toxicity and the larger application subject to certain restrictions, if Vc their combination, can reduce toxicity. New Jersey now Englehard company Hollis developed a cisplatin and Vc mixture composition which has better efficacy.

The whole plant contains Solasonine and solanine which also have activity against S_{180} sarcoma. Nigrum extract of dried green fruit of total alkali Solanum nigrum can inhibit animals transplanted tumor system by 40- 50%. In tissue culture 50-500mcg/ml 24h total alkali Solanum nigrum inhibit meningioma cells growth. Alkali component isolated from total alkali Solanum nigrum has the strongest antitumor activity and there are significant cytotoxicity. 10mcg / ml 15h concentration causes cells to collapse. A total extract also has inhibition effect on mice ascites sarcoma S_{180}. Solamine also be used as hematopoietic system stimulant, increasing leukocyte. barbata and comfrey it was used to treat malignant mole and the result is good. With surgery, chemotherapy, radiation it was used to treat uterine choriocarcinoma, -_in cancer, liver cancer and had effectiveness.

This product can inhibit cervical cancer U_{14} and S_{180}, Ehrlich ascites carcinoma and -hosarcoma, Ehrlich ascites carcinoma, L_{615} lymphatic leukemia, S_{180}, gastric cancer cells and leukemia in mice, etc

SNL has anti-cancer effect on nuclear division. Extract of SNL has inhibition rate of -50% on animal transplanted tumor. In tissue culture 50-50Oug/ ml 24 hr total SNL can inhibit brain tumor cell growth.

(4)

Anti-tumor components C: PGS saponin Ginsenoside
Formula formula :

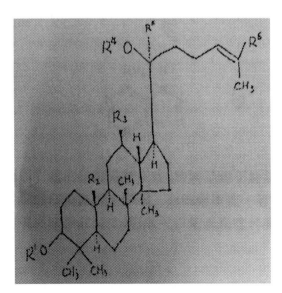

Anti-tumor effects:

On mouse sarcoma S_{180} it had significant inhibition at 120mg / kg/d x7 and the inhibition rate of its tumor weight was 60.48%; on Ehrlich ascites carcinoma (ECS) at a dose of I00mg / kg / d x70, its inhibition rate was 36.40%; on S_{180} at a dose of 100 mg / kg / dx10 its inhibition rate was 41-61% (P <0.05); large doses on U_{14} also have some anti-tumor effect.

With chemotherapy drugs CXT used in conjunction, it can enhance the anti-tumor effects of chemotherapy drugs.

Its anti-tumor effect is more complex; one, it can act directly with the cancer cell- -that the cancer cell growth was inhibited or be reversal. Second, it can also regulate the body metabolism and the immune function to resist diseases so that the tumor growth was inhibited. National and international clinical trials have proved: it has therapeutic effect on gastric cancer, not only reduces tumor; but also increases appetite, improves immunity and prolongs patients' survival time.

PGS soap component as a human anti-tumor agents, adapt to a wide range, almost no side effects. The application ranges: gastric cancer, colorectal cancer, breast cancer, uterine cancer, mouth, esophagus, gallbladder cancer, kidney cancer, lung cancer, brain cancer, liver cancer, skin cancer, etc., are valid for almost all tumors. The mode of administration: it can be taken orally at 100-300mg/ day x2-3 doses. It can also used 1-10% of hydrophilic or hydrophobic ointment topically.

Korea Atomic Energy Research Institute Nguyen and other reports: Application -- carcinogens in laboratory animals treated, serving long red ginseng can reduce the incidence of cancer and inhibit tumor growth. Small Tajima and other reports: cultured hepatoma cell PGS soap can change the cancer cell structures indicating PGS can induce cancer cells to be reversed. Hiroko Abe and other reports: PGS saponin induced reversal to hepatic cancer cells. Li xianggao believes: PGS soap can inhibit 3-O- methyl glucose through the cell membrane and overflow on liver cancer cells so presumably the inhibition of membrane transporters of PGS saponin may non-specific.

In addition to the relevant ginseng root soap antitumor activity studies, ginseng flower total inhibition has also been reported: Yuyongli and other scholars studied, the effect of a total ginseng flower soap on NKC-IFN-IL-2 regulatory network

and inhibition of tumor Effect. The results showed that: PGS total promote natural killer activity in vitro mouse spleen, and in the presence of Con-A induces the production of Y-IFN and IL-2, indicating the total soap flower PGS has regulation -KC-IFN-IL-2 network to regulate the immune function by this adjustment extensive network.

Liang Zhongpei etc applied PGS to study how dimethyl buttery yellow sugar induced rat liver cancer. The results showed that: PGS can increase the percentage of ANAE e lymphocyte cells, reduce the incidence of liver cancer, the tumor is smaller, a degree of differentiation of cancer cells, the longitudinal fibers hyperplasia and cute infiltration around tumor tissue, indicating that PGS should be able to promote immune function so that it has prevention or control action to the chemical carcinogen-induced liver cancer.

Ginseng inhibits variety of experimental animals. Ginseng had reduced tumor incidence nor growth inhibition after rats and mice were fed with ginseng long-term for aflatoxin-induced rat lung adenomas, urethane-induced lung cancer in mice. Its main anti-tumor ingredient is Ginseng saponin of which ginseng saponin Rg3 can - inhibit tumor formation of new organs, inhibit tumor recurrence, proliferation and metastasis in mouse melanoma and S_{180} tumor. The inhibition rate was 60% and on a variety of animal and human tumor lung metastasis, liver metastasis the inhibition ached 60% -70%. Ginseng saponin Rg3 is promising as anti-metastatic drugs.

(5) Z-C-E PCW

Antitumor points A, Adenine
Structure:

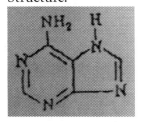

The presence of areas: plant sclerotia.

Anti-tumor effect: for the prevention and treatment of various leukopenia, particularly caused by chemotherapy, radiotherapy and benzene poisoning. Its phosphate stimulates - blood cell hyperplasia. It was found that Leukocyte recovered about 2-4 weeks after administration. It can extend the time of chemotherapy and prevent the occurrence of leukopenia if used before chemotherapy or simultaneously.

Anti tumor B: Pachyman
Structural formula:[13-D-Glcp- (1.-3) a 13-D.-Glcp- (1 - 3)] n

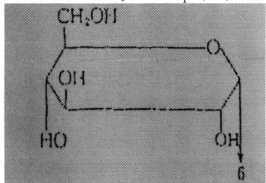

Antitumor effects: Studies have shown that: new Pachymaran: in 1970 Chihara etc slightly transform pachyman structure into pachymaran of removing the side chain β (1--6) with significant anti-tumor activity, but the poor water-soluble activity.

Carboxymethyl Pachymaran was synthesized by Hamuro etc. in 1971 with pachymaran carboxymethylation which has significant anti-tumor activity in animal experimeriments.

Hamuro, J and other experiments proved: new biological Pachymaran of pachyman such as CM-pachymaran and HM-pachyman 2-4, have significant anti-tumor actin activity of its agents and routes of administration have a great relationship and the appropriate route of administration of the optimal dose must be selected.

About pachyman antitumor mechanism of action and its derivatives, it has also reported: think no direct cytotoxicity; however through the host's intermediary it played anti-tumor roles which enhance the body's immune system.

Chaoqiaoli etc. observed inhibition of carboxymethyl Pachymaran mouse lung metastasis of inbred uterine cancer U_{615}. The results show that the non-transfer 64% tumor control group were 94%; metastasis inhibition rate of 75.68%, significantly higher than the control group, the experimental group tumor weight, inhibition rate was 23.58%, the above results suggest that: indeed carboxymethyl Pachymaran has some anticancer activity.

Data reported also: carboxymethyl tuckahoe polysaccharide is a good immune enham: and apply the treatment of various tumors.

Patent No. 4339435 reports: A Poria sclerotium obtained cultured mycelium, tilt-the mycelium of the water or that the water-soluble organic solvent such as ethanol extraction, to obtain an anti-cancer medicament "A-1", it is not only very good anti-cancer activity and no toxicity, 92% inhibition of the S_{180}, this anti-cancer substance accounted for 24.2% cultured mycelia. Xu Jin et al reported that a group of fat-soluble organic tetracyclic three, collectively known as Poria factors was isolated from Pachyman and significantly inhibited Ehrlich ascites carcinoma, S_{180} metastasis of Lewis lung carcinoma in mice. When administered with Cyclic amines and phosphorus, there is a certain synergy and it proved Poria increases immune function.

In 1986 Japanese scholars Jinshan isolated a water-soluble anti-tumor polysacchariL called Pachymaran H11 from cultured mycelia of Poria, accounting for about 0.69c dry mycelium. With 4mg / kg injection JCR / TCL mice subcutaneously x10 days S_{180} the inhibition rate was 94%, this report shows that there have been polysaccharide which has anti-cancer activity with no structural transformation in Poria.

There are also reports, after Poria cocos contained β - polyester (β -pachyman) was treated and approached to obtain Poria cocos glycan complex (abbreviated UP), it had a significant anti-tumor effect and the inhibition rate was 57%. It can extend tumor-mice survival time, improve the spleen index, and it has a direct effect on cancer cells.

Wu Bo and other scholars also conducted experiments to observe PPS's anti-tumor effect and mechanism on mouse S_{180} cells and human leukemia cells K5G2. It was that PPS has a strong suppression effect and discusses its anti-tumor mechanism of S_{180} cell membrane composition. The results showed that after PPS contacts with cells 24h, the membrane phospholipid content decreased and cell membrane sialic content increased, but the membrane cholesterol content, membrane fluidity membrane fatty acid composition is not affected. When PPS membrane put together with S_{180} under appropriate conditions, it was found that PPS interference of membrane of inositol phospholipid metabolism is critical step. Changes related to PPS antititumor mechanism and biochemical characteristics also have some reports. PPS significantly inhibited DNA synthesis in mouse L_{1210} cells with irreversible inhibition increased with the dose.

Poria has anticancer drug synergistic effect : on mitomycin and using inhibitory (mouse sarcoma S_{180}) was 38.9% (5-Fu alone 38.6%) ; in mouse leukemia L1210 cyclophosphamide alone amines life extension of 70%, combined with phosphorus domide was 168.1%.

PPS and thymus-related anti-tumor effect. Polysaccharides can nonspecifically stimulate the reticuloendothelial system function and enhance the host of cancer-specific antigen immunity to resist the effects of cancer.

Pachymaran with Poria known significant anti-tumor effect, can inhibit the growth solid tumors, extend survival time in mice S_{180} and Ehrlich ascites carcinoma. Pachymaran has distinct anticancer roles on cultured mouse sarcoma S180 cells and human chronic myelogenous leukemia K562 cell. Antitumor mechanism includes two aspects of increased immune system and direct cytokine roles. Antitumor mechanism y be suppressed by inhibiting tumor cell nuclear DNA synthesis and enhance production of tumor necrosis factor (TNF) from macrophage and the ability to enhance or cell killing effect.

Intraperitoneal injection of polysaccharides (PPS) 5-200mg / kg continuous 100, above 10mg, it inhibited S_{180} significantly. On S180 sarcoma in mice and Ehrlich ascites cinoma (EAC) orally taken 8d, it can enhance tumor necrosis factor (TNF) levels and significantly increase natural killer (NK) cell activity.

It significantly inhibited lung metastasis from U_{14} after mice were fed carboxymeth-. tuckahoe polysaccharide (250mg / kg/d) 25d. The mouse sarcoma S_{180} cells were seeded in ICR / JCL mice subcutaneously, 24 hours later 5mg / kg polysaccharides once daily once 10 days injected intraperitoneally. The results showed that inhibition rate was 95%.

Carboxymethyl Pachymaran strongly inhibited U_{14} in mice. Using 500mg / kg, 100mg / kg, 50mg / kg, the result of inhibition rate was 75.5%. 92.7% 78.7%, respectively, which 100 mg / kg dose was the best. Intraperitoneal injection carboxymethyl tuckah polysaccharide 100mg / kg/ d 10d extended lifetime was 23.49% compared with control in Ehrlich ascites carcinoma. It reduced the amount of ascites 7%, reduced total number of cancer cells 139.20%. PPS can inhibit DNA synthesis in Ehrlich ascites tumor cells. The inhibition role of PPS is related to the dose which using 100 / 50mg / kg, 5mg / kg 3 the results of tumor inhibition rates were 92.3%, 96.1%, 53.4%.

(6) Z-C1-G GuF

Anti-tumor components A: Glycyrrhiza acid
Structure:

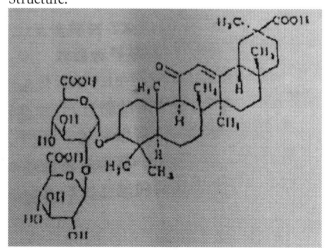

Existing parts: wooden grass roots, rhizomes.

Antitumor effects: The product can produce morphological changes on rat hepatoma and Ehrlich ascites carcinoma (EAC) cells and inhibit subcutaneous Yoshida sarcoma. Licorice as raw material soluble Monoaniniornum glycyrrhetate, namely licorice acid amine, can inhibit Ehrlich ascites carcinoma and muscle tumor. Meanwhile, licorice acid amine has some detoxification for certain toxic of anti-cancer drugs. Natural products such as having a certain anti-tumor effect: Caniptotliecine causes toxic reactions and limits the use of drugs, but a licorice acid amine can lower camptothecin toxicity by not reducing its efficacy and having a certain synergy. On animal experiments: the number of white blood cells caused by camptothecin, Glycyrrhizinate amine has protective effect.

This product is hot-water extract on human cervical cancer cells JTC-26 and inhibition rate is 70%- 90%.

Anti-tumor component B: Gycyrrhetinic aicd
Struture:

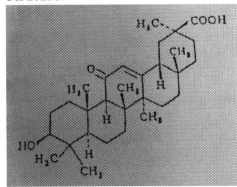

Existing parts: the herbal roots, rhizomes.

Antitumor effects: glycyrrhetinic acid inhibited transplanted Oberling-Guerin myeloma on rat. Its sodium salt has been inhibition on the growth of mouse Ehrhlich ascites carcinoma and sarcoma -45, even orally.

Anti-tumor components: Liguirtin
Structure:

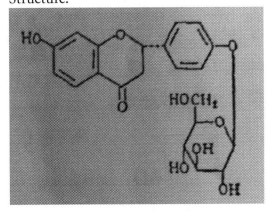

Existing parts: the root herbal.

Antitumor effects: The product can inhibit morphological changes and also have anti-rumor effect on rat hepatoma and Ehrlich ascites carcinoma cells and rat mammary tumor. It has the preventive effect on rat stomach cancer, can reduce the incidence of rastric cancer. In addition, grass sweetener has inhibited aflatoxin B1-induced hepatic precancerous lesion.

(7) Z-C-K LwF

Antitumor points: (Tetrainethylpyrazine, TTMP)

Anti-tumor effects: TTMP can inhibit TXA2 synthetase activity. Li Xue Tang et al reported: TTMP administered once has a certain anti-metastatic effect on hepatoma cell metastasis. Jin Rong and other reports: TTMP anti-tumor effect and its mechanism, the experimental results show that: TTMP at 20mg/d x 18d could significantly inhibit the artificial lung metastasis in B16-F10 melanoma and TTMP can enhance normal and tumor-bearing spleen NK cell activity in isotope incorporation assay in mice and antagonized cyclophosphamide inhibition of NK cell activity. TTMP anti-metastatic effect may be related to reduce plasma TXB content and to enhance NK cell activity.

Some academics have also been reported: isolated from this plant gland (Adenine), its pharmacological activity has been confirmed that stimulate white blood cell proliferation, prevent fine thrombocytopenia, particularly for leukopenia caused by radiotherapy or chemotherapy. TTMP has a certain anti-metastatic effect on liver cancer cells.

(8) Z-C-L AMB

Anti-tumor component B: p-Sitosterol
Structure:

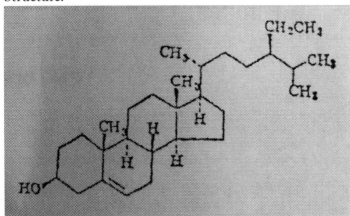

Existing parts: The root of the plant.

Anti-tumor effects: p-Sitosterol has an edge activity for lymphocytic leukemia P134; has effect on mouse adenocarcinoma 715, which inhibition rate of tumor weight (TWI) was> 58%; it has effects on Lewis lung carcinoma,its TWI was > 58%; for the rat carcinoma Wacker cancer 256 its TWI was > 58%.

Reports: AMB roots have in a certain amount of polysaccharide; AMB polysaccharide contains 1.34-2.04% and there are several polysaccharides. It has broad biological activity and has anti-tumor effect in vivo, but does not directly kill cancer cell in vitro which means that AMB polysaccharide works by enhancing immune function.

AMB can improve human and mouse plasma cAMP levels, can inhibit tumor growth, and make tumor cells even reversed; can promote animal leukocytosis; can recover leukopenia induced by chemotherapy or radiotherapy; can promote immune function and inhibit tumor cell killing effect. The inhibition rate of its water extract was 41.7% in vivo experiments on mice sarcoma -180. The alcohol extract AMB is currently used clinically as an anticancer drug righting.

ZhouShuYin reported: the results of AMB polysaccharide show in vivo experiments: APS 2.5mg/kg, 5mg/kg, 10mg/kg, 20mg/kg significantly inhibited on transplanted tumor S_{180} liver cancer; in vitro results showed that: APS and interleukin-2 can significantly improve the compatibility of applied rate LAK cell killing target cell P851 and Yae cells. Its anti-tumor mechanism is related to increasing immune function.

In vivo the inhibition rate of AMB hot extract was 41.7% on mice sarcoma S180; was 12.25% on human lung adenocarcinoma SPC-A- 1. The inhibition index Iodized oil was induced with MCA human-mouse lung which the injection group with MCA was 16.28%, the control group was 51.52% cancer, the difference is very significant. MCA can inhibit DNA synthesis in human ovarian cancer cells. When the concentration increases, the inhibition will strengthen and the duration of action of the drug will prolong and inhibition of DNA synthesis of cancer cells also will be enhanced. MCA polysaccharides have synergies on T lymphocyte activation at malignant ascites.

(9) Z-G-M LIA

Fight tumor components: Ursolic acid
Structure:

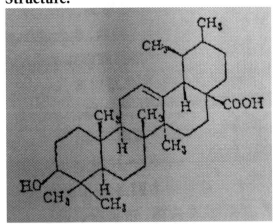

Exist parts: the leaves of the plant.
Anti-tumor effect: it has a very significant inhibition rate on cancer cells in vitro culture and can prolong the life on Hershey ascites carcinoma mice.

Pharmacological experiments show that: the goods flooding agent can inhibit certain animals transplanted tumor growth; it can increase immune function; it can recover leukopenia induced by chemotherapy and radiotherapy. There are also reported thr the active ingredient in this product is Oleanic acid.

(10) Z-C-N CzR

Anti-tumor component A: Turmeric alcohol Curcumol
Structure:

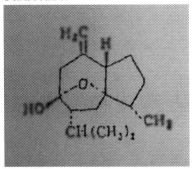

Exist parts: roots for the plants.

Anti-tumor effects: Curcumol has anti-tumor effect. At 75mg/kg the inhibition rate -Nis 53.47-61 .96% on mice sarcoma S37; at 75ug/kg the inhibition rate was 45.1-77.13% on mice cervical cancer U14; the inhibition rate was 65.8- 78.9% at the same doses on EAC. There is better effect on treating cervical cancer.

Antitumor Component B: Turmeric dione /Curdione
Structure:

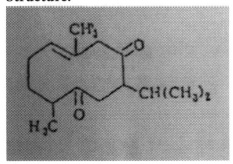

Exist parts: roots for the plants.

Antitumor effects: turmeric significantly inhibited mouse sarcoma 37, U_{14} and neck cancer and mouse Ehrlich ascites carcinoma and can make cancer cells degeneration end necrosis. After this product is processed in Ehrlich ascites carcinoma it can be successfully immunized mice to obtain initiative. The clinical results indicate that cervical cancer has a good effect.

There are also reports: In its same plant Curcuma wenyujin Y.H. Chen etc isolated β-elemene which has anti-cancer activity. The research proved that β-elemene could significantly prolong the survival time on Ehrlich ascites carcinoma and ascites reticulocyte cell sarcoma in mice and has strong killing effect on liver cancer cells in vitro. It also reduced nucleic acid content on EAC, especially in RNA content decreased more significantly. On leukocyte and bone marrow nucleated cells and Immune test: β-elemene has relatively small toxicity.

100% 0.3-0.5ml of Curdione has a good effect and the inhibition rate reached over 50% when it was injected to mice abdominal in S_{180}.

(11) Z-C-Q LBP

Antitumor components:. Lycium burbarum Polysaccharides LBP Structure: The main components are arabinose, glucose, galactose, mannose, xylose, rhamnose and other components. Exist parts: to have come from the fruit.

Anti-tumor effect: Wangbekung etc proved: LBP enhanced immune function on normal mouse cells. At 10mg / kg it can improve the immune function and have inhibitory effect on S180 tumor-bearing mice, and synergistic anti-tumor effect with chemotherapy cyclophosphamide. There are also reports: LBP has a certain influence on the immune function. Lu Changxing and other reports: LBP showed significant radiosensitization with radiotherapy.

In addition, its roots and skins have Betaine, which also have anti-cancer function: with D-isoascorbic together it can inhibit mitosis in vitro on sarcoma 37, Ehrlich cancer and lymphoid leukemia L1210 which is stronger than alone medication. LB P contained (3- sitosterol, ascorbic acid, etc. which has anti-tumor effect.

There are also reports: LBP and interleukin-2 have the regulation effect on two anti-tumor LAK activity.

(12) Z-C-R

Panax pseudo-Wall, var.notoginseng Hooet Tseng
Anti-tumor components: Notoginsenoside R1
Effective parts: that the roots of plants.
Antitumor effects: 180 μg/ml 5 days Panax saponin R can induce 68% HL-60 cell differentiation which proved Panax saponin R1 is a strong inducer of HL-6 0 cell lines and can induce HL-60 neutrophil cell differentiation. H-TdR incorporation assay results show: notoginsenoside R1 can induce differentiation of HL-60 cells while it affects DNA and RNA synthesis. There are also reports: during Cr release assay with soap studied Panax test it induced mouse spleen activity against tumor; have a strong anti-tumor effect with ConA / PHA together. Further experiments showed that soap Panax has no stimulation on proliferation of splenocytes, but changes the level of intracellular CAMP in spleen cells.

(13) **Z-C-Z1**

Corioius versicolor Quel.

Anti-tumor components: Polysocohaitibe-piptide

Structure: a, R (1-4) dextran as main chain of Polysaccharide with 15% protein and kinds of amino acids

The presence of site: mycelium body

Antitumor effects: target cells: human gastric cancer cell lines (SGC7901); hum:- lung adenocarcinoma fine lines (SPC); human monocytic leukemia cell line (SLY human skin cell lymphoma cell lines (MEI)

In vitro inhibitory test of PSK Application the results showed that: PSK has moderate inhibition of proliferation at a concentration dose 1000ug / ml on human lung adenocarcinoma cell line (SPC). The Japanese scholars shared PSK (Kiestin) has effects on sarcoma 180, liver AH-13, AH-7974, AH-66F, leukemia P388 in vivo by intravenous, intraperitoneal, subcutaneous, or oral administration and has almost no toxicity. Its mechanism is to improve the immune function through "host agency" role.

Li Jian and other scholars in the report: versicolor extract has no inhibition on ascites hepatoma on subcutaneously transplanted mouse while it has significant effects on the subcutaneous mouse ascites sarcoma S_{180}.

In clinical the extracellular polysaccharide PSK is used on primary liver cancer and alone n improve the clinical symptoms and prolong life, anticancer drugs; in combination with antitumor drugs it also reduces the toxic side effects of antitumor drugs. Japanese vood has developed into proteoglycan "PSK" anti-cancer drugs.

(14) **Lentinus edodes Sing**

Anti-component A: Lentinan

Structure: The structure of p-D- (1 3) glucan backbone, C-6 has two fulcrum of every D- glucosyl, connecting p-D- (1 6) and p-D- (13) glucose branched-chain, also containing small amounts p-D- (16) branches.

Existing parts: its fruiting bodies.

Anti-tumor effects: Lentinan has some anti-tumor effect and improve the body's immune function. At a dose of 0.2, 1, 5, 25mg /kg, the daily cavity injection for consecutive 10 days, the inhibition rates were 78, 95.1, 97.5 and 73% on S180. It can Increase their compatibility of anti-tumor effect with chemotherapy drugs.

Lentinan can induce DNA synthesis and immune globulin and interferon-inducible, and non-specific cell-mediated cytotoxic effect in human peripheral mononuclear cells (PMNC, mainly lymphocytes); can enhance the cytotoxic response of NK cells of NK cell activity is very low and even absent in Leukemia patients; the general immune enhancer treatment increases the risk of cancer of the white blood cells. Lentinan can Increase the activity of NK cells. It induced β-IFN which has stronger anti-cancer effect than α and β -IFN, can enhance the phagocytic activity of white blood cells in patients with hormone production. At the same time, it can prevent patients with cancer from bacteria and viruses infection.

Shiio T et al reported: LNT and chemotherapeutic agents together can inhibit tumor metastasis in mice which the effect is the best when it is administrated after the surgery. Fachet T et al found Lentinan and their preparations A/ph(A/ph B10) F1hybrid mice A/ph, MC, S1 fibrosarcoma have significant anti-tumor alivity; however, Lentinan does not directly affect tumor growth in vitro. Shiio T et al also studied the inhibitory effect of Lentinan on cancer lung metastasis; intravenous Lentinan can inhibit Lewis system cancer (3LL), melanoma (B6) and fiber sarcoma (ML-CS-1) metastasis.

10

The exclusive research and development products: a series of products of Z-C immune regulation of anti-cancer Chinese medication (Introduction)

Exclusive research and development of products: XZ-C immunomodulatory anticancer medicine products (Profile)

Independently developed XZ-C (XU ZE China) series of anti-cancer immune regulation medicine preparation, from experimental research to clinical validation, in animal experiments on the basis of success in clinical practice, clinical experience over the years a large number of clinical cases verification, a significant effect. The results are self-invention, the Department of independent innovation and intellectual property rights.

The research of Looking from traditional Chinese medications, and screening anti-cancer, anti-metastatic new drug:

The purpose is to screen out non-resistance, non-toxic side effects, a high selectivity, long-term oral anti-cancer, anti-metastatic and anti-recurrent cancer drug. It is well known now for the world's anti cancer agent docs inhibit proliferation of cancer cells, but it only kill cancer cells but also kill normal cells, especially the bone marrow of immune cells, a host of serious damage, because of chemotherapy cytotoxic and non-selectivity. And traditional chemotherapy can suppress the immune function and inhibit bone marrow function. Traditional intravenous chemotherapy treatment is interrupted, the cancer cells cannot be treated during the gap period which cancer cells continued proliferation and division. Although chemotherapy drugs can inhibit the proliferation of cancer cells, but because of its toxic side effects when cancer has not yet been eliminated, administration had to stop. After treatment, cancer cell proliferation up again, and began to have resistance. When resistance, this dose would not work so as to increase the amount executioner. However, if the dose is increased, it may endanger the lives of patients. If the chemotherapy drug resistance has been given, then the cancer is not only ineffective; Contrary to killing only patient's normal cells so cancer cells resistance to cancer drugs and toxics of cancer drugs on the host side effects is a long vexing problem. And we are looking for new drugs, the purpose is to avoid these drawbacks.

According to the theory of cell cycle, anticancer agents must be able to continue long applications so that cancer foci can bath in anti-cancer agents long lasting time, and is available without stopping

41

to prevent their cell division and to prevent recurrence and metastasis. Must be long years, have been conducting long-term, it is best to long-term oral drugs to control existing foci and prevent nascent cancer cells to form. Due to large toxicity the currently used anticancer medication cannot long continuous use, but only short cycle applications. Existing anticancer medication has suppressed immune function, bone marrow suppression, suppression thymus, bone marrow suppression side effects. The formation and development of cancer is due to the patient's immune system to reduce lost immune surveillance, therefore, all anticancer medications should be increased immunization, protection immune organs, immune suppression and should not use drugs.

To this end, we conducted the following experiment laboratory screening of new anti-cancer research from the traditional Chinese medicine, anti-metastatic drugs:

A. **The method of cancer cells in vitro, the experimental study of Chinese herbal medicine suppressor screening rates:**

In vitro screening tests: The cancer cells in vitro was observed for sore drugs directly damage cells.

Screening in vitro culture of cancer cells in vitro tests respectively allowing raw and crude drugs of crude product (500ug / ml) to be used and to observe whether there is inhibition of cancer cells, we believe that 200 kinds of traditional Chinese medicine herbs have anticancer function performed one by one in vitro screening tests. And under the same conditions with a normal fiber cell culture to test the toxicity of these cells, and then compared.

B. **Building cancer-bearing animal model for the screening of Chinese herbs for cancer-bearing animal experimental tumor suppressor rate**

Suppressor in vivo screening test, each batch experiments with mice 240, divided into 8 groups, each group 30, the first group was the control group 7, group 8 with 5-Fu or CTX control group, the whole group of small mice was inoculated with EA C or S 180 or H22 cancer cells. After inoculation 24h, each rat oral feeding crude product of crude drug powder, long-term feeding the screened the herbs, observed survival, toxicity, computing prolong survival rate calculated suppression sores.

So, we conducted experimental study for four consecutive years, and has conducted a 3-year incidence of tumor-bearing mice and transfer mechanism, the experimental study of the mechanism of relapse, and experimental studies to explore how cancer causing death of the host each year with more than 1,000 tumor-bearing animals model, made a total of nearly four years, 6000 tumor-bearing animal models, mice each were carried out after the death of the liver, spleen, lung, thymus, kidney pathological anatomy, a total of 20,000 times slice to explore to find out whether There may be slight carcinogenic pathogens, with microcirculation microscope 100 tumor-bearing mice were tumor microvessels bell establish and microcirculation.

Through experimental study we first found in China a medicine to inhibit tumor angiogenesis TG had a significant effect, more than 80 cases have been used in clinical treatment of patients Hang metastasis being observed.

42

Results: In our laboratory animal experiments screened 200 kinds of Chinese herbs and screened48 kinds of certain and excellent herbs with inhibition of cancer cell proliferation, inhibition rate of more than 75 to 90%. But there are some of commonly used Chinese medicine which consider to have the anticancer roles, after animal in vitro and in vivo inhibition rate anticancer screening, showed really no effect, or little effect which 152 kinds of medications having no anti-cancer effect had removed from the phase-out of animal experiments.

Screening out of this real 48 kinds of traditional Chinese medications with having good tumor suppression rates, and then optimized the combination and repeated tumor suppression rate experiments in vivo, and finally developed immunomodulatory anticancer Chinese medication XU ZE China1-10 with Chinese own characteristics China (ZC $_{1-10}$).

Z-C$_1$ could inhibit cancer cells, but does not affect normal cells; Z-C$_4$ specially can increase thymus function, can promote proliferation, increased immunity; Z-C$_1$ can protect bone marrow function and to product more blood.

Clinical validation: Based on the success of animal experiments, clinical validation was conducted. Namely the establishment of oncology clinics and Western medicine combined with anti-cancer, anti-metastasis, recurrence Research Group, retained patient medical records, to establish a regular follow-up observation system to observe the long-term effect · face from experimental research to clinical evidence, the discovery of new clinical validation process issue, went back to the laboratory for basical research, then the results of a new experiment for clinical validation. Thus, a clinical experiment again and again clinical experiment, all experimental studies must be clinically proven in a large number of patients observed 3--5 years, or even clinical observation of 8 to 10 years, according to evidence-based medicine, and can have long-term follow-up assessment information, verified indeed have a good long-term efficacy, the efficacy of the standard is: a good quality of life, longer survival. XZ-C sectional immune regulation anti-cancer medicine made after a lot of applications in advanced cancer patients verification, and achieved remarkable results. XZ-C sectional immune regulation anti cancer medicine can improve the quality of life of patients with advanced cancer, enhance immune function, increase the body's anticancer abilities, increased appetite and significantly prolong survival.

C. **XZ-C immunomodulatory anticancer Chinese medication Mechanism of Action**

With the deepening of traditional Chinese medicine research, it is known to produce a lot of traditional Chinese medicine and biological activity of cytokines and other immune molecules having a regulatory role, this time to clarify XZ-C from the molecular level immunomodulatory anticancer Chinese medication immunological mechanisms very important.

1. XZ-C immunomodulatory anticancer Chinese medication can protect immune organs, increasing the weight of the spleen and chest pay attention.
2. XZ-C immunomodulatory anticancer Chinese medication for hematopoietic function of bone marrow cell proliferation and significant role in promoting.
3. XZ-C immunomodulatory anticancer Chinese medication on T cell immune function enhancement effect on T cells significantly promote proliferation.

4. XZ-C immunomodulatory anticancer Chinese medication for human IL-2 production has significantly enhanced role.

5. XZ-C immunomodulatory anticancer Chinese medication activation of NK cell activity and enhance the role, NK cells with a broad spectrum of anticancer effect, can anti-xenograft tumor cells.

6. XZ-C immunomodulatory anticancer Chinese medication for LAK cell activity can enhance the effect, LAK cells are capable of killing of NK cell sensitive and non-sensitive solid tumor cells, with broad-spectrum anti-tumor effect.

7. XZ-C immunomodulatory anticancer Chinese medication to induce interferon and pro-inducing effect, IFN has a broad-spectrum anti-tumor effect Wo immunomodulatory effects, IFN can inhibit tumor cell proliferation, IFN can activate the skin to kill cancer cells and OIL cells.

8. XZ-C immunomodulatory anticancer Chinese medication for colony stimulating factor can promote credit enhancement, CSF not only involved in hematopoietic cell proliferation, differentiation, and in a host of anti-tumor immunity plays an important role

9. XZ-C immunomodulatory anticancer Chinese medication can promote tumor necrosis factor (TNF) role, TNF is a class can directly cause tumor cell death factor, its main biological role is to kill or inhibit tumor cells.

D. **Bilogical response modification(BRM), traditional chinese anticancer medicine similar to BRM and tumor treatment**

1. **Biological reaction modification (BRM) explores the new field of the tumor biological therapy. Currently BRM as the fourth methods of the tumor treatment gets widely attention in the world.**

Oldham in 1982 built BRM theory. Based this in 1984 he advanced the fourth modality of cancer treatment-----biological therapy again. According to this, in the normal condition, there is the dynamic equilibrium between the tumor and the body. The development of the tumors, and even invasion and metastasis, completely is caused by the loss of this equilibrium. If this unbland situation is adjusted to the normal level, the tumor growth can be controlled and will disappear.

The anticancer mechanism of BRM in details as the following:

(1) Improve the host defence abilities or decrease the immune inhabitation of the tumors to the host to reach the immune response to the tumors.

(2) Look for the biological active things in natural or gene combination to enhance the host defense abilities.

(3) Reduce the host response induced by the tumor cells

(4) Promote the tumors to division and mature to become the normal cells

(5) Reduce the side effects of the chemotherapy and redio therapy and enhance

The host toleration.

2. XZ-C immune regulation anticancer medicine have the functions and curative effects similar to BRM

After four years experimental research and 16 years clinical research which are the drugs similar to BRM selected from traditional Chinese medicine.

XZ-C is the drugs that XU ZE in China professor selected from two hundreds of the anticancer herbs after the experiments. At first the culturing tumor were done. The in vitro was done One by one to select and abserve the direct damage to tumor cells in the culture setting and the control groups of the rate of the anticancer are the chemotherapyxxxx and the normal culture tube cells. The results are to select the a series of the medicine of the anti-cancer proliferation, then made the animal modes which 200 drugs were used on one by one. These experiments of the analysis and evaluation are steps by steps, scientific, practical and strict, etc. The results proved that48 of them have the excellent tumor inhibition effects, however the rest 152 of the tumors anticancer medicine are all common old anticancer medicine which proved no anticancer or less inhibition of the tumors in the animal models during these medicine selection experiments.

The medicine which the author selected on the tumor animal models and had excellent anticancer rat XZ-C can improve immune function, protection of the central immune organs such as thymus and, improving the cell-mediated immune functions, protecting the thymus function, protect the bone morrow function, increase the red blood cells and white blood cells number, active the immune factors, improve the immune surveilence in the blood ect.

XZ-C the main anticancer pharmacology function si anticancer and increase of the immune function. The above XZ-C has the following function as :

(1) Activing the host immune system to promote the host immune function to reach the immune respond to the tumors.
(2) Activing the host immune factors of the anticancer systems to strengthen the host immune function and improve the immunce surviellence of the host immune systems.
(3) Protecting the thymus and bone marrow, improve the immune system, and stimulate the bone marrow function to reduce the inhibition of the bone marrow and increase the white blood cell and red blood cells etc.
(4) Reduction of the side effects of the chemotherapy and radioactive therapy to increase the tolerance of the hosts.
(5) Increaseing thymus weight and stop the shrinkle of thymus because when the tumor develop thymus goes on shrinkles.

As mentioned above, the mechanism of action of z-c immunomodulation anticancer Chinese medicine is basically similar to BRM. Clinical application also results in the same therapeutic effect of BRM. Therefore, z-c immunomodulation anticancer Chinese medicine has a BRM-like effect and efficacy and is the combination of today's advanced molecular oncology theory with ancient Chinese herbal medicine resources at the molecular level, Western medicine. Using BRM theory as a bridge is in line with the advanced theory and practice of international modern molecular oncology.

A. XZ-C1 "Smart grams cancer"

The main components are eight Chinese herbs.

Anticancer pharmacology

1. Detoxification, increasing blood circulation, righting, dispelling evil without injury, strong inhibition of cancer cells and inhibition of cancer cell metastasis without inhibition of normal cells.
2. In anti-cancer in vivo tests in mice, they have inhibitory activity in the mice Ehrlich ascites tumor cells which there had been significant differences in the control group.
3. Can prolong survival of mice bearing cancer, increased the survival rate of 26.92%.
4. The main prescription drugs Z-C1-A and Z-C1-B has a stable and significant anticancer effects, 100% inhibition of cancer cells, cancer cell mitotic reduced and degenerated and necrosed seriously and epithelial cells or fibroblasts is no impact in the administration group. XZ-C1-D extract have inhibitory activity on human cervical cancer cells, on mouse sarcoma s180 inhibition rate was 98.9%, several other ingredients also have a strong anticancer effect.
5. Z-C1 Herbs inhibition effect on Mice bearing H22 hepatoma tumor: z-c1 drug inhibition rate was 40 percent in the second week, the first four weeks was 45%, the first six weeks of 58%; in the control group CTX medication first two weeks inhibition rate was 45%, the first four weeks inhibition rate was 45%, 49% for the first six weeks.
6. Z-C1 medicine influence on survival in mice bearing H22: life-prolonging rate was 85% in z-c1 group; life extension was 9.8% in CTX control group ; in Z-C1 group Thymus did not shrink; however thymus shrank in Control group.

Clinical application

1. Indications: esophageal cancer, stomach cancer, colorectal cancer, lung cancer, breast cancer, liver pain, bile duct cancer, pancreatic cancer, thyroid cancer, nasopharyngeal cancer, brain tumors, renal cancer, bladder cancer, ovarian cancer, cervical cancer, various sarcoma and a variety of metastasis, recurrent cancer.
2. Usage: after taking z- c1 continuously 1 - 3 months, the patients felt better. This medication can be taken for long-term and can be taken one dose every other day after three years; can be taken two doses weekly after 5 years to retain immune function and cytokine long-term stable at a certain level.

Toxicity Test

ZX-C1 can be used for long-term. The acute toxicity test showed that when adult mice was fed a dose 104 times (10g / Kg body weight), respectively, in 24, 48, 72, 96 hours of observation, 30 purebred mice didn't die. The median lethal dose (LD5O) didn't have any number so that it is a rather safe prescriptions.

In the oncology clinic it has been used for many years and some patients have taken more than three to five years and more than 8 to 10 years in order to maintain immunity and to stop recurrence. It can be taken for long-term and it is quite safe oral cancer.

B. **XZ-C2**

Ingredients: 9 kinds of anticancer herbs

Anticancer pharmacology

1.   Animal experiments show that it can prolong L7212 mouse (mouse leukemia) survival, well-behaved compared to the control group, there were statistically significant.
2.   Can improve inhibition rate in the L7212 in mice
3.   Z-C1-A and Z-C2-B on mouse sarcoma (s180) has a strong inhibitory effect.

Application

Indications: leukemia, upper gastrointestinal cancer, tongue, larynx, nasopharynx cancer, cervical cancer, bone metastasis, esophagus cancer or gastric ulcer anastomotic recurrence narrow (no longer surgery). It has general effect on Acute leukemia lymph and has obvious efficiency of each of the other type of leukemia. It has a more significant effect on Bone metastasis

Usage: one capsule Qid generally or two capsules tid

Leukemia 3 capsules tid after meal and seven days for a course.

C. **XZ-C3 topical pain Patch**

Prescription Content: kaempferol, turmeric, etc. 14 flavors

Anticancer pharmacology

1.   Detoxification, anti-inflammatory pain, qi Sanjie pain;
2.   Increasing the blood circulation, reducing swelling and pain, played a total of detoxification, swelling and analgesic effect, while the most prominent role in cancer treatment is to stop pain.
3.   For point application, applicator than simply pain, can better play the efficacy and achieve rapid pain relief purposes.

Clinical application

Indications: liver cancer, lung cancer pain, back pain from pancreatic cancer, bone pain, neck and supraclavicular lymph nodes metastasis.

Usage: A total of research and go take honey, mix, stir into a paste backup, lung disease spreads in milk root point (nipple straight down 5, 6 ribs), liver cancer spreads on the door hole (milk midline 6-7 rib room), treated and covered with gauze and tape securely, severe pain 6h for a second, lesser pain, 12h replacement of 1: continuous use to relieve pain or disappeared.

Experience: Treatment of 84 cases of liver cancer, lung cancer pain patients, have analgesic effect, general medicine three times, will receive different levels of pain relief, 3 to 7 days after a significant analgesic effect, some basical pain.

D. **ZX-C4 anticancer medication of protecting thymus and increasing immune function (5g / bag)**

Ingredients: including 12 valuable herbs

Anticancer pharmacology

1. To promote lymphocyte transformation, enhancing immune function, increased white blood cells, inhibit cancer cell, Warming blood.
2. Ehrlich ascites tumor cells transplanted into the abdominal cavity of mice, one day after transplantation and 7 Days 2 times for chemotherapy drugs in mice, while serving z -c4 (2g / kg) per day is significantly enhanced the effectiveness of chemotherapy drugs effect.
3. To suppress leukopenia and weight loss induced by chemotherapy medicinal MMC MMC
4. While serving Z-C4, it was found to inhibit cancer cells in terms of improving the effect of intravenously injected anticancer chemotherapy drugs than simply using more than three times in cancer-bearing mice.
5. Chemotherapy drugs for cancer-bearing mice can damage special thymus, spleen and other immune organs, but after adding the service z-C4, thymus, spleen and other organs completely don't shrink, showed z-C4 have effects on the immune organ protective nature function.
6. ZX-C4 extract in Ehrlich ascites disease mouse prolonged the mice life span of up to 167.1%, the average survival time of mice in the control group 15.2 days, and z-c4 administration group is 25.4 days, while reticuloendothelial system function in mice showed significantly higher.
7. Z-C4 allows the chemotherapy drugs cisplatin quickly to mitigate its effects, can enhance the effectiveness of cisplatin. z-C4 can be 100% inhibition of cisplatin toxicity chloroplatinic day conventional dose amount that is human can be. z-c4 not resist cisplatin Chen Hang crazy. z-c4 can protect the kidney, the renal damage cis-platinum chlorine hardly occurs. Z-C4 has highly promising anticancer drug.

8. Z-C4 patients after cancer surgery have a significant effect, gastrointestinal, liver, pancreas and other ulcer disease after radical: all manifestations of physical decline, decreased immunity, fatigue, burnout, loss of appetite and anemia, after 1 a 2 weeks from the beginning can be oral or tube feeding, oral Z-C4 granules, 7.5 g daily, before meals three times a blunt, 12 weeks, during which can be chemotherapy or immune therapy.

9. Z-C4 medicine antitumor effect in mice bearing hepatoma H22: z-C4 first two weeks of medication inhibition rate was 55%, the first four weeks inhibition rate was 68%, the first six weeks inhibition rate was 70% the control group, CTX (cyclophosphamide Yu amine) Week 2 inhibitory drugs was 45%: the first four weeks inhibition rate of 49%.

10. z-C4 medicine for liver cancer H22 bearing mice survival, z-C4 group extend survival rate 200%, CTX group life span was 9.8%.

11. Z-C4 can significantly improve immune function, can increase white blood cells and red blood cells, liver and kidney function had no effect on the liver, kidney slices without damage. CTX cause leukopenia, reduced immune function, kidney sections have kidney damage.

12. Z-C4 treated group Thymus do not shrink and slightly hypertrophy, CTX thymus control group significantly shrink. Z-C4 on mouse sarcoma (S180) has a strong inhibitory effect.

Clinical Application:

Indications: various types of cancer, sarcoma, a variety of advanced cancer, metastasis, recurrence of cancer, radiotherapy, chemotherapy, post-operative patients. It can be applied all kinds of cancer, especially dizziness, weakness, fatigue, lazy words, less gas, spontaneous sweating, heart palpitations, insomnia, blood deficiency were more applicable.

Z-C4 medicine was used before surgery and after starting the medication and medication every four weeks to do a clinical and laboratory tests, for 20 weeks. Test items: conscious and objective symptoms, body weight, total protein and albumin, total cholesterol, dielectric, ALT AST blood and platelets, lymphocytes, T cells and B cells, r globulin, urinary protein.

Treatment Results: ① increase in the number of lymphocytes, inhibit the role of leukopenia; ② no impact on liver function; ③ protect the kidney function, kidney damage is not so; ④ can significantly reduce the chemotherapy and radiotherapy-induced rash, stomatitis etc; ⑤ postoperative, after chemotherapy, effective physical recovery after radiotherapy, can increase appetite, improve the general malaise and weight gain.

ZX-C4 reduce side effects of radiotherapy and chemotherapy and improve the overall state of the patient after surgery. It is a very valuable rehabilitation medication.

Experience: Modern medicine for the treatment of advanced cancer presents a variety of methods, but there are still some problems, it is still not convinced that the combined use of chemotherapy for advanced disease if certain effective drugs. Even if effective, but it also brings serious side effects, may be considered modern medical treatment for cancer is to kill cancer cells, is offensive, while the Chinese places to enhance the body's own functions to draw even tone pull eliminate cancer. To this end, it should find a way to reduce or eliminate symptoms, improve or treat the disease with few side effects, the treatment can prolong life, and Z-C4 being has the features and advantages.

Through experiments ZX-C4 has the role of enhanced anticancer effect ; promote B cell mitosis role; the catch into the effects of radiation damage hematopoietic system recovery; the promotion of the role of phagocytic cells; thymus increased protective immunity, protection of bone marrow Blood role.

Toxicity Test

Z-C4 can be used long-term. Acute toxicity experiments showed that the median lethal dose (LD50) can not do, is safe and herbs, has been used in the specialist clinic for many years, some patients long-term use three to five years, or even take 8-10 years to maintain immunity, prevent cancer recurrence and metastasis. This anticancer and antimetasatasis medication can be taken by oral for long-term oral and is quite safe.

E. **The following XZ-C various immunomodulatory anticancer medicine series and the experimental and clinical contents are too many and too long so that here only gave names and profiles were omitted.**

1. XZ-C5:for liver cancer
2. XZ-C6: for bladder cancer
3. XZ-C7: for Lung cancer
4. XZ-C 8: protect bone marrow and increase blood, attenuated toxics of radiotherapy and chemotherapy
5. XZ-C9:pancreas cancer, prostate cancer.
6. XZ-C10: for brain tumor

All of above of a variety of cancer anticancer, antimetastasis, recurrent research Chinese medicine are based on the experimental study and applied by specialist in outpatient clinics more than 20 years and achieved good results.

Our research Chinese medications for cancer complications in out-patient center of cancer treatment:

1. Anticancer eliminate water soup for pleural effusion and ascites
2. Drop yellow soup for liver cirrhosis and jaundice
3. Anticancer soup after surgery for postoperative recovery
4. Starvation soup for cancer loss of appetite
5. Through Quiet soup for anastomotic stenosis
6. Adhesiolysis soup for adhesions after surgery for cancer

Above all research product formulations. Observation by cancer specialist clinic over the years on many patients, have achieved good results, reduce patient suffering, improving the survival quality first, extended survival.

A series of products of XZ-C immunoregulation anti-cancer traditional Chinese medicine

1. **XZ-C1+4: for all kinds of cancer**
2. **XZ-C1: has the stable and significant anti-cancer effects, the inhibition rate up to 98%, no harmful to normal cells.**
3. **XZ-C4: protection of thymus and increase of immune function, promote the thymus proliferation, increase the immune function XZ-C8: protection of bone marrow and production of blood, increase T cells, and anti-metastasis**
4. **Lung cancer: XZ-C1+XZ-C4+XZ-C7**
5. **Breast cancer: XZ-C+XZ-C+XZ-C+ mushroom**
6. **Esphogus cancer: XZ-C1+XZ-C4+XZ-C2**
7. **Stomach cancer: XZ-C1+XZ-C4 or +XZ-C5**
8. **Liver Ca: XZ-C1+XZ-C4+XZ-C5 + Mushroom+ Red ginseng**
9. **Bile cancer: XZ-C1+XZ-C4+XZ-C5 + Capillaris**
10. **Pancrease cancer : XZ-C1+XZ-C4+XZ-C5+XZ-C9**
11. **Colon and rectal cancer: XZ-C1+XZ-C4+XZ-C5**
12. **Kidney and bladder cancer: XZ-C1+XZ-C4+XZ-C6**
13. **Cervical and ovary cancer: XZ-C1+XZ-C4+XZ-C5+ Lms+ MDS**
14. **Lymphma: XZ-C1+XZ-C4+XZ-C2+ Dai Dai**
15. **Leukemia: XZ-C1+XZ-C4+XZ-C2+XZ-C8+ barge pole**
16. **Prostate cancer:XZ-C1+XZ-C4+XZ-C6**

Comments: A series of XZ-C immune regulation anti-cancer traditional medications have been verified and tested for 20 years in Shuguang tumor special out-patient center on 12,000 of middle or later stage cancer patients. On clinical application they can change the symptoms, the patients have the good spirit and appetites are good, the life quality is improved, and they significantly prolong the survival time.

Adaptation Scope of Clinical application observation of XZ-C immunomodulation Chinese medication XZ-C$_{1-10}$ anti-cancer metastasis and recurrence

1. a variety of distant metastatic cancer, such as liver metastases, lung metastases, bone metastases, brain metastases, abdominal lymph node metastasis, mediastinal lymph node metastasis, cancerous pleural effusion, cancerous ascites, can be applied XZ-C immunization Regulate and Control anti-metastatic treatment, according to the transfer step, intervene and block the cancer cells on the way to prolong life.

2. After all kinds of radiotherapy and chemotherapy have been completed, XZ-C1-4 should be taken to control the traditional Chinese medicine to consolidate the long-term effect and prevent recurrence.

3. in the process of radiotherapy and chemotherapy, if the reaction is serious and can not continue, you can continue to use XZ-C immunomodulation therapy to resist metastasis and recurrence.

4. in the elderly or weak patient with other diseases who cannot have radiology and chemotherapy, XZ-C immunomodulation anti-metastasis, relapse treatment.

5. surgical exploration can not be cut, can be used XZ-C immune regulation treatment.

6. after palliative surgery, XZ-C immunomodulation anti-metastatic treatment.

7. after a variety of cancer radical surgery, should continue to take XZ-C immunomodulation treatment of traditional Chinese medicine anti-recurrence, metastasis, in order to improve the long-term effect after radical surgery

Summary table of the main pharmacological effects of Z-C immune regulation anticancer Chinese herbal medicine (anti-cancer and increasing immune)

	Increased white blood cells	Enhanced phagocytosis	Enhance cellular immune	Enhance humoral immune	Enhanced hematopoietic function	Improve gastrointestinal function	(count)	Enhance the weight of the thymus	Promote bone marrow cell proliferation	Enhanced T cell function	Enhanced NK cell activity	Enhanced LAK cell activity	Enhanced IL-2 activity levels	Enhance the level of interferon IFN activity	Enhanced TNF activity levels	Enhanced CSF colony stimulating factor	Antagonistic WCBYC ↓	Inhibition of platelet coagulation and antithrombosis	(count)	Antitumor	Anti-metastasis	Antiviral	Anti-cirrhosis	Liver protection	Eliminate free radicals	Protein synthesis	Anti-HIV	(count)
Z-C-A-APL																				+	+							
Z-C-B-SLT																				+	+							
Z-C-C-SNL																				+	+							
Z-C-D-PGS	+	+	+	+	+	+	6	+	+	+	+		+	+	+	+	+		9	+	+	+			+	+		20
Z-C-E-PCW		+	+				2	+	+				+	+	+	+	+		7	+	+	+						12
Z-C-F-AMK		+	+	+	+	+	5		+				+			+			3	+		+		+				11
Z-C-G-GUF		+	+	+		+	4				+		+					+	3	+		+		+		+		11
Z-C-H-RGL	+		+		+		3	+	+				+	+		+			5	+					+			10
Z-C-I-PLP	+	+	+	+	+	+	6	+	+									+	3	+		+					+	12
Z-C-J-ASD	+	+	+	+	+		5	+	+	+			+	+	+		+	+	8	+					+			15
Z-C-K LWF		+	+				2								∣			+	2	+	+							5
Z-C-L-AMB	+	+	+	+	+		5	+	+	+	+	+	+	+					7	+		+				+		5
Z-C-M LLA	+	+	+	+			4	+		+									2	+						+		5
Z-C-N-CZR		+					1							+				+	2	+	+							5
Z-C-O-PMT	+	+	+	+	+	+	6	+	+	+						+			4	+		+	+	+	+	+		16
Z-C-P-STG							0												0	+								1
Z-C-Q-LBP	+	+	+	+	+		5		+	+	+	+	+		+	+	+		8	+	+				4			16
Z-C-R-NSR		+					1	+			+						+		3	+	+		+	+				8
Z-C-S-GLK	+	+	+	+	+		5		+		+	+	+		+	+			6	+	+			+		+	+	16
Z-C-T-EDM	+	+	+	+	+		5	+		+			+	+	+	+			6	+		+		+				14
Z-C-U-PUF		+	+	+			3		+	+	+								3	+				+				8
Z-C-V-ABB							1		+	+	+		+						4	+								6
Z-C-W-SCB	+						1	+									+		2	+					+	+		5
Z-C-X-SDS							0				+	+	+						3	+								4
Z-C-Y-PAR							0				+	+	+		+	+			5	+								6
Z-C-Z-CVQ							0								+				1	+								2

11

The Research on Action Mechanism of Xz-C Traditional Chinese Anti-Carcinoma Medication With Immunologic Regulation and Control

With more and deeper researches on traditional Chinese medicine, it has been proved that many kinds of traditional Chinese medicine can regulate and control the production and biological activity of cytokine and other immune molecules, which is meaningful to explain the immunological mechanism of XZ-C traditional Chinese anti-carcinoma medicine for immunologic regulation and control from the level of molecule.

I.   XZ-C anti-cancer medications can protect Immune Organs and Increasing the **Weight of Thymus and Spleen**

That XZ-C traditional Chinese medicine can protect immune organs resulting from the following active ingredients or principles.

1. XZ-C-T (EBM):

Using its 15g/kg and 30g/kg extracting solution (equivalent to 1g original medicine) along with 12.5mg/kg, 25mg/kg ferulic acid suspension to feed the mice for seven days in a raw can **increase the weight of thymus and spleen obviously**, especially the effects of the group with high dose are more apparent. Intraperitoneal injection of EBM polysaccharide can also alleviate thymus and spleen atrophy obviously caused by perdnisolone.

2. XZ-C-O (PMT)

Extract PM-2, feed the mice with 6g/(kg·d) PMT decoction for successive seven days which can increase the weight of thymus and celiac lymph nodes and antagonize the reduction in the weight of immune organs caused by perdnisolone. Drenching the mouse of 15 months old with 6g/kg decoction (with the concentration of 0.5g/ml) for 14 days can increase the **weight and volume of thymus, thicken the cortex and raise cellular density apparently**. The combined use of PM and astragalus root can promote non-lymphocyte hyperplasia and benefit the micro environment of thymus.

3. XZ-C-W (SCB)

SCB polysaccharide **can gain weight of thymus and spleen of a normal mouse**. Lavage with it enables cyclophosphane to control the gain in the weight of thymus and spleen.

4. XZ-C-M (LLA)

Drench a mouse with LLA decoction for seven days resulting in increasing the weight of thymus and spleen.

5. XZ-C-L

For a 15-month old mouse, its thymus degenerates obviously. Astragalus injectio can enlarge the thymus significantly. The cortex under microscope is thickened and the cellular density increase obviously.

II. <u>Effects on Proliferation, Differentiation and Hematopiesis of Marrow Cells</u>

The following active principles of XZ-C traditional Chinese medicine have effects on hematopiesis of marrow cells.

1. XZ-C-Q (LBP) extracts (PM-2)

(1) Effects on the proliferation of hematopoietic stem cell (CFU-S) of a normal mouse: inject PM-2 with the dose of 500mg/(kg·d)×3d or 10mg/(kg·d)×3d LBP into the experimental mice respectively by venoclysis and kill them in the ninth day. It can be found that the number of spleen CFU-S in the group with administration increases obviously. The number of CFU-S in group PM-2 is 21% higher than that of the control group and it is 36% in the group with LBP.

(2) Effects on colony forming unit of granulocytes and macrophages (CFU-GM): the experimental results indicate that LBP with the dose of 5~30mg/(kg·d)×3d can increase the number of CFU-GM and PM-2 can also strengthen the effect of CFU-GM with the effective dose of 12.5~50mg/(kg·d)×3d. In the early stage of cultivation, most CFU-GMs are units of granulocytes and then units of macrophages increase gradually. In the anaphase units of macrophages take over the dominance.

From the above experiment, it can be found that PM-2 and LBP can promote hematopiesis of normal mice obviously. The experiment proves that during the process of restoring hematopiesis damaged by cyclophosphamide, PM-2 and LBP stimulate the proliferation of granulocytes at first, and then marrow karyocytes multiply; at last these two promote the restoration of peripheral granulocytes.

2. XZ-C-D (TSPG)

Ginsenoside, which is the active principle of ginseng to promote hematopiesis, can bring the recovery of erythrocyte in peripheral blood, haemoglobin and myeloid cell of thighbone in the mice of marrow-inhibited type, increase the index of myeloid cellular division and stimulate the proliferation of myeloid hematopoietic cell in vitro so as to make it into cell cycle with active proliferation (S+G_2/M stage). TSPG can promote the proliferation and differentiation of polyenergetic hematopoietic cells and induce the formation of hemopoietic growth factor (HGF).

3. XZ-C-H (RCL)

Steamed Chinese Foxglove can promote the recovery of erythrocyte and haemoglobin for animals with blood deficiency and accelerate the proliferation and differentiation of myeloid hematopoietic cell (CFU-S) with the effect of predominance and hematosis significantly. Peritoneal injection of rehmannia polysaccharides for successive six days can promote the proliferation and differentiation of myeloid hematopoietic cells and progenitor cells as well as increasing the number of leucocytes in peripheral blood.

4. XZ-C-J (ASD)

ASD polysaccharide has no effects on erythrocytes and leucocytes of normal mice, but for those damaged by radiation, injection of ASD polysaccharide can influence the proliferation and differentiation of both polyenergetic hematopoietic stem cells (CPU-S) and hemopoietic progenitor cells. But its decoction has no obvious effects.

5. XZ-C-E (PEW)

Poria cocos (micromolecule chemical compound extracted from Tuckahoe polysaccharide) is the active principle that can strengthen the production of colony stimulating factor (CSF) and improve the level of leucocytes in peripheral blood inside the mouse's body. It can also prevent the decline in leucocytes caused by cyclophosphamide and accelerate the recovery with the effects better than sodium ferulic which is used to increase leucocytes.

6. XZ-C-Y (PAR)

Its polysaccharide can obviously resist the decline in leucocytes caused by cyclophosphamide and increase the number of myeloid cells to promote the proliferation of myeloid induced by CSF as well as the recovery and reconstitution of hematopiesis for the mice irradiated by X ray. It can also increase the number of hematopoietic stem cells and myeloid cells along with leucocytes.

III. **Enhancing Immunologic Function of T Cells**

The active principles of XZ-C traditional Chinese medicine and their effects are following.

1. XZ-C-L (AMB)

It can raise the percentage of lymphocytes in peripheral blood obviously. The LBP in small dose (5~10mg/kg) can cause the proliferation of lymphocytes, indicating that LBP can promote the proliferation of T cells apparently. 50mg/(kg·d)×7d is the best dose in that it will have no effects if lower than the level and it will bring the effects down if higher than the level. Oral administration of LBP can raise the conversion rate of lymphocytes for the sufferers who are weak and with fewer leucocytes.

2. XZ-C$_4$

It can regulate immune system and active T cells of aggregated lymphatic follicles, as well as stimulate the secretion of hemopoietic growth factor in T cells. Among the crude drugs of XZ-C$_4$, the extract from the hot water of atractylodes lancea rhizome can obviously stimulate the cells of aggregated lymphatic follicles, which is regarded as the base of XZ-C$_4$ immunoloregulation.

IV. **Activating and Enhancing NK Cell Activity**

Natural killer cell, NK cell is another kind of killer cell in lymphocytes for human beings and mice, which needs neither antigenic stimulation, nor the participation of antibodies to kill some cells. It plays an important role in immunity, especially in the function of immune surveillance as NK cell is the first line of defense against tumors and has broad spectrum anti-tumor effects.

NK cell is broad spectrum and able to kill sygencous, homogenous and heterogenous tumor cells with special effects on lymjphoma and leucocytes.

NK cell is an important kind of cells for immunoloregulation, which can regulate T cells, B cells and stem cells, etc. It can also regulate immunity by releasing cytokines like IFN-α, IFN-γ, IL-2, TNF, etc.

The active principles in XZ-C traditional Chinese medicine and their effects are following.

1. XZ-C-X (SDS)

Divaricate Saposhniovia Root can strengthen the activity of NK cells of experimental mice. When combined with IL-2, it can make the activity of NK cell higher, indicating that its polysaccharide can give a hand to IL-2 to activate NK cells and improve the activity.

LBP can strengthen T cell mediated immune reaction and the activity of NK cells for normal mice and those dealt by cyclophosphamide. Peritoneal injection of LBP can improve the proliferation of spleen T lymphocytes and strengthen the lethality of CTL increasing the specific lethal rate from 33% to 67%.

2. XZ-C-G (GUF)

Glycyrrhizin can induce the production of IFN in the blood of animals and human beings and strengthen NK cell activity at the same time. Clinical tests made by Abe show that after intravenous injection of 80mg GL, the raise of NK cell activity reaches 75% among 21 sufferers. Peritoneal injection of 0.5mg/kg GL on mice can strengthen the activity of NK cells in liver.

3. XZ-C-L (AMB)

Its bath fluid can promote NK cell activity of mice both in vivo and in vitro, and can also induce IFN-γ to deal with effector cells under the certain concentration of 0.1mg/ml. Cordyceps sinensis extract can strengthen NK cells activity of the mouse both in vivo and in vitro. Fluids with the concentrations of 0.5g/kg, 1g/kg and 5g/kg can strengthen NK cell activity of mice.

V.   Effects on LAK Cell Activity

Lymphokine activated killer cell, namely LAK cell can be induced by IL-2 cytokine. LAK cells can kill the solid tumors that are both sensitive and insensitive to NK cells with broad anti-tumor effects.

The active principles in XZ-C anti-carcinoma traditional Chinese medicine and their effects are following.

1. XZ-C-L (AMB)

Its polysaccharide can strengthen LAK cell activity within a certain range of dose with 0.01mg/ml being the most effective, which is three times better than the damage effects of LAK cells. The concentrations of both higher and lower than this level can not achieve the effects.

2. XZ-C-U (PUF)

It can significantly strengthen the spleen LAK cell activity of killing tumor cells and improve the activity of erythrocyte C3b liquid. PUF and IL-2 are synergistic that can be used as regulator for biological reaction in tumor biological therapy based on LAK/Ril-2.

3. XZ-C-V

ABB polysaccharide can also raise LAK cell activity for the mouse and inhibit tumors remarkably. Its anti-tumorous mechanism relates to its strengthening immunity and changing cell membrane features.

VI. **Effects on Iterleukin-2 (IL-2)**

The active principles in XZ-C anti-carcinoma traditional Chinese medicine and their effects are following.

1. XZ-C-T

EBM polysaccharide can enhance obviously the production of IL-2 for human beings when the concentration is 100ug/ml. At higher concentration (2500ug/ml and 5000ug/ml), it will lead to inhibition. Hypodermic injection of barrenwort polysaccharide for seven days in a row can significantly improve the ability of thymus and spleen of the mouse induced by ConA to produce IL-2.

2. XZ-C-Y

PAR polysaccharide has strong immune activity and is able to promote the production of IL-2. For the mouse bearing S-180 tumor, it can raise the ability of spleen cells to produce IL-2 obviously。

3. XZ-C-D

Ginseng polysaccharide has great promotion on IL-2 induced by peripheral monocytes for both healthy people and sufferers with kidney troubles. The effects are relevant to the dose positively.

VII. **Function of Inducing Interferon and Promoting Inducement of Interferon**

IFN are broad-spectrum in resisting tumors and can regulate immunity. It can also inhibit the proliferation of tumor cells and activate NK cells and CTL to kill tumor cells. Meanwhile, IFN can cooperate with TNF, IL-1 and IL-2 to enforce anti-tumorous ability.

The active principles in XZ-C anti-carcinoma traditional Chinese medicine and their effects are following.

1. XZ-C-Z

250mg/kg or 500mg/kg CVQ polysaccharide can improve significantly the level of IFN-γ produced by mouse spleen cells.

2. XZ-C-D

Ginsenoside (GS) and panaxitriol ginsenoside (PTGS) can induce whole blood cells and monocytes of human beings to produce IFN-α and IFN-γ. It can also recover the low level of IFN-γ and IL-2 to the normal.

The IFN potency of ASH polysaccharide on S-180 cell line of acute lymphoblastic leukemia and S_{7811} cell line of acute myelomonocytic leukemia produced after acanthopanax polysaccharide stimulation is 5~10 times more than that of normal control group.

3. XZ-C-E

Hydroxymethyl Poria cocos mushroom polysaccharide has many kinds of physical activity like immunoloregulation, promoting to induce IPN, resisting virus indirectly and alleviating adverse reaction resulting from radiation. Do IFN inducement dynamic experiment on S-180leukaemia cell line by using 50mg/ml Hydroxymethyl Poria cocos mushroom polysaccharide. The results indicate that its potency to induce interferon at all stages is better than that of normal inducement.

4. XZ-C-G (GL)

It can induce IFN activity. Make peritoneal injection of 330mg/kg GL on mice. IFN activity reaches the peak after 20 hours.

VIII. Function of Promoting and Increasing Colony Stimulating Factor

Colony stimulation factor, namely CSF is a kind of glucoprotein with low molecular weight that can stimulate the proliferation and differentiation of marrow hematopoietic stem cells as well as other mature blood cells. Cells that can produce CSF include mononuclear macrophages, T cells, endothelial cells and desmocytes. CSF not only take part in the proliferation and differentiation of hematopoietic stem cells and regulating mature cells, but also play an important role in anti- tumorous immunity of host cells.

The active principles in XZ-C anti-carcinoma traditional Chinese medicine and their effects are following.

1. XZ-C-Q

PAR polysaccharide is able to promote to produce CSF by spleen cells of experimental mice. 100~500ug/ml PAP-II can encourage spleen cells to produce CSF depending on the dose and time with the fittest dose of 100ug/ml and best time of 5d. Moreover, lentinan can also increase the amount of CSF.

2. XZ-C-Q

Injection of LBP can facilitate the secretion of CSF by mouse spleen T cells and improve the activity of CSF in serum.

3. XZ-C-T

EBM icariin can promote the proliferation of mouse spleen lymphocytes induced by ConA and bring CSF activity.

IX. **Function of Promoting TNF**

Tumor necrosis factor, namely TNF is a kind of cytokine that can kill tumor cells directly. Its main effect is to kill or inhibit tumor cells, which can kill some tumor cells or inhibit the proliferation both in vivo and in vitro.

The active principles in XZ-C anti-carcinoma traditional Chinese medicine and their effects are following.

1. XZ-C-Y (PEP)

It can induce the production of TNF, so as PEP-1. Inject 80~160mg/kg PEP-1, once every four days. Collect peritoneal macrophages (PM), add 10ug LPS into culture medium to cultivate PM. Take the supernatant to determine TNF and IL-1. It can be found that PEP-1 can parallelly increase the auxiliary production of TNF and IL-1. The time of TNF inducement reaches the peak on the 8th day after the second intraperitoneal injection. Compared with the known startup potion BCG, the inducement of TNF has no difference.

2. XZ-C-E

Carboxymethyl-pachymaran (CMP) is the principle essential component distilled from traditional Chinese medicine Tuckahoe. It can not only strengthen the ability of mouse spleen to create IL-2 and macrophages and promote the activity of T cells, B cells, NK cells and LAK cells; but also encourage the production of TNF. The experiment proves that CMP is an effective potion to promote and induce cytokines.]

3. XZ-C-V

ABB polysaccharide can promote the production of TNF-b in mouse cells induced by ConA. It can also induce the synthesis of peritoneal macrophages and secrete 20ug/ml TNF-α achyranthes bidentata polysaccharides. The time of TNF-α to reach its peak is 2~6 hours after effects. Peritoneal injection of 100mg/kg achyranthes bidentata polysaccharides can accelerate the production of TNF-α, whose intensity of effects is comparable to that of BCG.

X. **The effects on Cell Adhesion Molecule**

Most adhesion molecules are glycoproteid and are distributed on cellular surface and extracellular matrix. Adhesion molecules take effect in the corresponding form of ligand-acceptor, resulting in the adhesion between cells, or between cell and stroma, or the adhesion of cell-stroma-cell. These molecules take part in a set of physical pathologic processes, like cellular conduction and activation of information, cellular stretch and movement, formation of thrombus as well as tumor metastasis, etc. Intercellular adhesion molecule-1, namely ICAM-1 is one kind of adhesion molecules in the super family of immune globulins.

The effect of corn stigma as an active principle in XZ-C traditional Chinese anti-carcinoma medicine: Hobtemariam has proved that alcohol extract from corn stigma has significant inhibition on the adhesion of endothelial cells to inhibit effectively the expression of ICAM-1 and the adhesive activity with TNF, LPS as agents.

12

The Survey of Research on XZ-C Immunologic Regulation and Control Medication

I.   The Experimental Research

In 1985, the writer made system follow-up statistics to more than 3,000 patients who had accepted cancer operations of chest and abdomen performed by the writer himself. The results show that 2-3 years after the operation, most patients suffer from relapses or metastases. To reduce the relapse rate and increase the curative rate, the clinical fundamental research is a must. If there is no breakthrough of fundamental research, the clinical effect is hard to improve.

Current anti-cancer drugs are cell toxicants that kill both cancer cells and normal cells. The untoward reaction is intense. Now a kind of anti-cancer drug is extracted from traditional Chinese medicine, such as vinblastine, which is extracted from vinca rosea as alkaloid, has been used as anti-cancer drugs for clinical practice. But it will also kill normal cells. So the untoward reaction is intense too. While we hope that anti-cancer drugs have fewer untoward reactions, may be taken by mouth and can build up patient's strength and resistance. Then scientific research is being designed. The plan is to adopt animal experiments of tumor-inhibition in tumor-bearing mice, and from natural drugs to find new anti-cancer drugs, anti-metastasis and anti-relapse drugs, traditional Chinese medicine that only inhibit cancer cells but not normal cells, and new drugs that can adjust the regulation and control relation between host and tumor.

According to cell proliferation cycle theory, anti-cancer drugs must maintain long-term application and make cancer nidi chronically and continuously immerse in drugs. Only in this way can the cell division be inhibited and relapse and metastasis be prevented. Drugs have to be used for a long term, which is the only way to control existing cancer nidi and prevent the formation of nascent cancer cells. But current used anti-cancer drugs induce intense untoward reaction, and therefore they cannot be used chronically and continuously but only be applied as per the treatment course for a minor cycle. All the current anti-cancer drugs have a series of untoward reactions, such as suppressions of immunologic function, bone marrow hematopoietic function and thymus gland, etc. the formation and development of cancer is due to the loss of immune monitoring caused by the reduction of patient's immunity. Therefore, all the anti-cancer drugs must improve immunity and protect immune organs, but should not suppress immunity.

To this end, our laboratory has carried on the following experimental studies for screening of new anti-cancer and anti-metastasis drugs from traditional Chinese medicine.

1. **Adopt the method of cancer cells cultured in vitro to carry on the screening experimental study of tumor inhibition rate of traditional Chinese medicine**

Screening test in vitro: adopt the method of tumor cells cultured in vitro; observe drugs' direct damage to tumor cells.

1. Method

(1) Preparation of crude drugs' agentia: dry crude drugs; add sixty times of water; heat and extract filtering liquid; decompress filtering liquid; distill it to dryness; form coarse dust; then it can be applied.

(2) Screening test in culture dish: 1×10^5 /ml cells of Ehrlich ascites tumor (FAC), or fleshy tumor 180 (S-180), or ascites liver cancer (H_{22}), or carcinoma of uterine cervix, fetal calf serum 10%, coarse crude drugs 500μg/ml, based on the above proportion to inject 20ml solution in culture dish of 10cm×15cm. Place it at 37 centi- degree for a given time. Then compare the quantity of surviving cells with those of control group. Measure suppression ratio of cell proliferation caused by cytotoxicity.

(3) Drug screening: put crude drugs respectively into test tubes that used for culturing human cancer cells. Observe them whether crude drugs have inhibiting action on cancer cells. For 200 kinds of anti-cancer traditional Chinese medicines identified by traditional Chinese doctors, the writer carries on the in vitro screening test in sequence. Also under the same condition, use those medicines to carry on fibrocytes culture of normal person. Measure this medicine's cytotoxicity to fibrocytes, and then compare it with that of control group.

2. The Experimental Result after animal screening tests by the writer in laboratory, 48 kinds of crude drugs (totally 200) certainly have and even hold sovereign inhibiting action on cancer cells proliferation. Tumor inhibition rate is above 90%. But some commonly used traditional Chinese medicines, which are generally considered to have anti-cancer effects, are verified by experiments to have no or little anti-cancer effects. The suppression ratio of another 50 kinds of traditional Chinese medicines is below 30%, such as Chinese clematis, selfheal, earth worm, akebia stem, cortex lycii, rosa multiflora and so on.

2. **Make animal model, carry on the experimental research of tumor inhibition rate of traditional Chinese medication in cancer-bearing animals**

1. The screening test of tumor-inhibition in vivo tumor-bearing animal model:

Each batch of experiment needs 240 Kunming mice, divided into 8 groups. Each group has 30 mice. For the first, second, third, fourth, fifth and sixth experimental group, each group chooses one kind of traditional Chinese medicine. The seventh group is set as the blank control group. The eighth group selects fluorouracil or cyclophosphamide as control group. All the mice are inoculated with 1×10^7 /ml EAC or S-180 or H_{22} cancer cells through right front axillary subcutaneous injection. After three days, green gram-sized subcutaneous tumor nidi grow. 24 hours after inoculation, each mouse is fed orally with coarse dust of crude drugs, as per the weight 1000mg/kg. The feeding time is once a day for eight weeks. Mice's weights and sizes of tumor nidi need to be measured daily. After eight weeks, 20 mice of each group are executed. Measure their weights of body, tumor, liver, spleen, lung, thymus gland and other organs. Make pathological section to observe tissue condition and know metastatic condition. Another 10 tumor-bearing experimental mice are chronically fed with the screening traditional Chinese medicine. Observe the surviving time and untoward reaction. Calculate prolonged survival rate and tumor inhibition rate. Each batch (i.e. screen each kinds of traditional Chinese medicine) of experimental cycle is three months. Each batch of experiments can simultaneously screen and study six kinds of traditional Chinese medicines or prescriptions. One group of experiments can simultaneously get screening results of six kinds of traditional Chinese medicines.

This research institute can test three experimental groups over the corresponding period. Three master or doctor postgraduates manage one experimental group. In this way can tumor inhibition experiments with eighteen single traditional Chinese medicines or prescriptions be simultaneously studied. In this year, 72 kinds of single traditional Chinese medicines screening experiments which are used for in vivo tumor-inhibition of tumor-bearing mice can be carried on and completed. Thus the writer has continuously carried on four-year experimental studies and another three-year study on pathogenesis and metastatic compound mechanism of tumor-bearing mice and exploration of reasons that why cancerous protuberance can cause the death of host. 1000 tumor-bearing animal models are used every year. A total of about 6,000 tumor-bearing animal models have been done during four years. Each experimental mouse is performed with pathological anatomy on liver, spleen, lung, thymus gland and kidney after death. More than twenty thousand pathological sections have been accomplished to explore and seek cancerogenic micro-pathogens. Use microscopes to observe tumor micrangium establishing and microcirculation condition of 100 tumor-bearing mice. Through experimental studies, the writer firstly finds in China that traditional Chinese medicine TG has obvious effects on suppressing the formation of tumor micrangium. Now this medicine has been used for clinical anti-metastasis treatments on over 200 patients. Curative effects are being observed.

2. Discussion

(1) Through experimental studies, put forward new thought, new knowledge, new concept and new strategy for resisting against cancer: over a period of seven years; over 6,000 tumor-bearing animal models; in vivo tumor-inhibition experiments for anti-cancer, anti-metastasis and anti-relapse in sequence with 200 kinds of natural traditional Chinese medicines; have cognizance of train of thought, knowledge and experience to renew concept, thought, traditional principle and method for traditional anti-cancer work.

Use tumor-bearing animal models to carry on scientific, objective and strict experimental screening, analysis and evaluation on 200 kinds of traditional Chinese medicines in sequence with so called anti-cancer curative effects by Chinese Medicine Literature. Results show that only 48 kinds of medicines have better anti-cancer effects. Although another 152 kinds of medicines are the commonly used anti-cancer medicines by veteran practioner of TCM, they have been verified by this group of experimental screenings to have no anti-cancer effects or little tumor inhibition rate. These 200 kinds of traditional Chinese medicines used for experimental screening are chosen from over ten books with TCM anti-cancer famous prescriptions. They are also common medicines with anti-cancer effects described in Journal of Traditional Chinese Medicine and literature reports. While the experimental study results prove that 152 kinds of medicines have no tumor inhibition rate or low anti-cancer effects. The reason might be that Chinese Medicine Literature has no distinction between lump, abdominal mass of Chinese medicine and cancer of modern medicine. 48 kinds of medicines in this group, which are screened through animal experiments, really have better tumor inhibition rate. Through optimization grouping and repeated trials, different medicines are composed to XZ-C$_{1-10}$ immunoregulation anti-cancer Chinese material medica preparation. It has been verified clinically for sixteen years. Over 12,000 cancer patients have used this preparation and obtained better curative effects.

Through experimental screening study results of this group, we have realized that TCM prescriptions are gained from prolonged experience. The prescription matches symptoms of disease and is the synthesis composed with various kinds of crude drugs. As seen from Chinese Medicine Literature, symptoms of abdominal mass and accumulation seem similar to those of cancer. Traditional Chinese medicines are used to treat abdominal mass. Sometimes symptoms can be improved, but not all abdominal mass are cancers. In general, TCM has no effect on cancer. So we should adopt modern scientific methods to verify, observe and reevaluate cancer resistance and carcinogenicity of various crude drugs in prescriptions of traditional Chinese medicine, and avoid unscientific parts of traditional Chinese medicine and pharmacology.

In medicine screening experiments, it's found that single crude drugs have worse tumor-inhibition effects than optimization grouping compound of many kinds of crude drugs. The reason may be that single crude drugs can only suppress tumor proliferation. While optimization grouping compound of many kinds of crude drugs not only can suppress tumor proliferation of tumor-bearing mice, but also can build up strength, improve immunity, promote to produce cancer-inhibition cytokines and protect normal cells.

Since 1992, over seven-year scientific experiments, different medicines are screened and composed to XZ-C$_{1-10}$ immunoregulation anti-cancer Chinese materia medica preparation. This medicine owns curative effects on anti-cancer, supporting healthy energy to eliminate evils, clearing away heat and toxic materials and activating blood circulation to dissipate blood stasis.

From experimental study to clinical verification, and then from clinic to experiment again, the writer has organized to set up the joint breakthrough research coordination group for cancer prevention and resistance. This coordination group has experimental study base and verification base of clinical application. The former is in medical college and medical university laboratory; the latter is in clinical medical department of nationwide coordination group for cancer prevention and resistance studies combined with traditional Chinese and western medicine. From experimental study to clinical verification means the clinical application on the basis of successful experimental study. Then new problems are found during the clinical application, which need fundamental experimental studies. Afterwards new experimental results are applied to clinical verification. Experiments → clinic → experiments once more → clinic once more, recurrent ascent continuously; through eight-year clinical practical experiences, knowledge also continues to improve. Summation, analysis, reflection and evaluation ascend to theory, putting forward new knowledge, new concept, new thought, new strategy and new therapeutic route and scheme.

Breakthrough research experience of coordination group includes:

① Choose the way that professors, experts and postgraduates of universities and colleges coordinate to carry on scientific researches and joint breakthrough; advocate large-scale coordination of scientific researches; give prominence to concentrate scientific research and technology strength of all parties; enrich anti-cancer strength.

② Cancer prevention and anti-cancer should make use of nation-wide advantages; give full play to the advantage of traditional Chinese medicine; conform to actual conditions in China.

③ Fundamental studies are important, but application and development research are more important. It should be observed that fundamental research → applied research →development research. Emphases are application and curative effects. Focus on increasing life quality of cancer patients, improving symptoms and prolonging survival time.

④ Restore the conservation of outpatient records (since 1976, Hubei province cancels conservation system of outpatient records and sends them to patients.); fill in full and detailed outpatient records. Therefore, full information of clinical verification is obtained to be convenient for analysis, statistics and follow-up survey (Generally, 80%~90% patients accept outpatient service, 10%~20% patients receive hospital treatment. At present hospital records are reserved to analyze and study clinical data. That 80%~90% patients accept outpatient service leads to the inexistence of outpatient records. Analysis, statistics and follow-up survey of patients' curative effects in out-patient department, and follow-up statistics of scientific researches may become impossible. Hospital records can only observe short-term curative effects; while the conservation of outpatient records can observe long-term curative effects.) Restoring and reserving outpatient records data is favorable toward outpatient clinical research to improve medical quality.

(2) Experimental work of finding new anti-cancer drugs, anti-metastasis and anti-relapse drugs from natural drugs:

it's aimed at screening new anti-cancer drugs with non-tolerance, no untoward effect and high selectivity that can chronically be taken by mouth. As known to all, although current anti-cancer drugs can suppress cancer cells proliferation, due to their severe untoward effect, while using many patients have to stop administration. Afterwards cancer cells proliferate again and begin to have drug tolerance. Such as the famous anti-cancer drug formyli sarcolysine quinine, as seen from ongoing cancer cells tissue cultures, drug tolerance is up to 20,000 times. Before the appearance of drug tolerance, the dosage is usually only several milligrams. While when drug tolerance is produced, such dosage cannot meet the demand. Then it is necessary to increase the dosage. But when its dosage increases to ten times, it will cause the death of patient. Therefore, drug tolerance of cancer cells on anti-cancer drug and untoward effect of anti-cancer drug on host are long-standing problems that puzzle tumor treatment researchers. Our purpose of finding new drugs is to avoid those disadvantages and screen anti-cancer drugs with non-tolerance, no untoward effect and high selectivity that best can chronically be taken by mouth. Western anti-cancer drugs have single ingredient. Micro dosage is effective, but it will suppress normal cells. Its toxic reaction is quite strong. Some current anti-cancer drugs are extracted from traditional Chinese medicine, such as vincristine, camptothecin and colchicine; these alkaloids are similar to traditional anti-cancer drugs, i.e. micro drug is effective, but toxicity is very high.

The question is whether anti-cancer traditional Chinese medicine, which can suppress the growth of cancer cells but not kill normal cells, can be extracted from TCM. Through several years' experimental screening, the writer finally finds such kind of TCM with rather ideal anti-cancer effects. Usually when the dosage reaches $500\mu g/ml$, it has inhibiting action on cancer cells. The writer also finds $XZ-C_1$ and $XZ-C_4$ drugs that can 100% suppress cancer cells and never kill normal cells. $XZ-C_1$, $XZ-C_4$ and $XZ-C_8$ also can improve the immunologic function of host, which is a superior feature of anti-cancer TCM.

As seen XZ-C series of TCM, its anti-cancer effect changes as the change of dosage. When the dosage is $250\mu g/ml$, it can only suppress 60% cancer cells; when the dosage is $125\mu g/ml$, suppression ratio is zero. Micro A-type drugs will be effective, such as vinblastine, berberine in Chinese goldthread, and myrobalan fruit in alkaloid, etc. But they can also suppress normal cell proliferation, which is same to traditional anti-cancer drugs. B-type drugs are other anti-cancer TCM. Only high concentration is effective. That is, micro dosage has no inhibiting action on cancer cells. Effect is directly proportional to dosage. If the dosage is larger, curative effects will be better, such as $XZ-C_{1A}$ and $XZ-C_{1B}$.

3. Verification of clinical effects

Over the past ten years, the writer has applied experimental crude drugs to clinical medicine. XZ-C series drugs have distinctive clinical effects. That is, a certain period after the administration of B-type drugs, cancer cells neither proliferate nor shrink, while the patient begins to restore vigorous energy. Several months later, the physical strength recovers gradually. The tumor starts to shrink slowly. That is probably not toxic effect on cancer cells, but the result of creating a circumstance that is adverse to cancer cells proliferation in organisms. The long-term administration has no toxic cumulative effect on normal cells. Many patients have taken XZ-C_1 and XZ-C_4 drugs for 3-5 years, there is still no relapse, metastasis and untoward effect. The long-term plentiful administration can obtain unexpected good results.

Different types of XZ-C preparation match with various kinds of cancers, such as cancer of alimentary canal, lung cancer and cancer of uterus, etc. Compound prescriptions must be made from symptoms. Only in this way can good results be obtained.

Different from traditional medicinal broth, what the writer chooses is the mixture with every kind of single crude drug through 100 mesh screening. These crude drugs are composed as compound prescription, which is not the decoction of combined preparation, but is the mixed preparation. This kind of mixture can preserve pharmacological characteristics of each crude drug. Prolonged use of this drug will not produce the untoward effect. Probing into the application way of crude drugs is quite significant.

In actual clinical medicine, will the prolonged use cause any problems? Patients can be divided into two kinds of cases: one type of patients take considerable amount of drugs with no abnormalities. The curative effects appear slowly. Many patients have taken XZ-C$_4$ drugs for 3-5 years. They have high spirits and good appetites. Physical strength recovers better; body condition strengthens; state of an illness is stable; patient's condition is good. The daily clinical dosage is about 20g of coarse drugs, in which the basic remedy is anti-cancer drugs, accounting for about 10% (equal to 40g crude drugs). It is considerably different from the dosage of traditional Chinese medicine.

When will curative effects present after taking medicine? Usually 1-3 months reach peak. Therefore if patients can survive for more than six months, then about 90% patients' symptoms can be improved remarkably; 50% patients' cancer proliferation will stop; about 80% patients' survival time is lengthened.

The completely significant thing is that XZ-C$_{1-4}$ crude drugs preparations have favorable abirritation. Medium and advanced stages of liver cancer and cancer of pancreas both produce severe pain. Patients who have used this kind of crude drugs preparation for over one month hardly feel any pain. They even don't have to be injected with analgesic drugs. This is extremely amazing.

Extracts of single crude drugs and compounded crude drugs almost produce the same curative effect. But when decocted with traditional compound prescription, extracts of single crude drugs are less effective. Presumably this is caused by the existence of interaction among drugs. In terms of cancer treatment, the better choice is compounded medicinal preparations.

Please note that some crude drugs can also promote the reproduction of cancer cells but suppress normal cells' growth, especially mineral drugs and animal drugs. Such as pallas pit viper, hairy antler and others, even the microdosis can promote above reactions. The centipede can damage renal tubules.

Akihiko Sato says that cancer resistance of natural drugs can be divided into three categories. The first category is that ingredients of natural drugs have the effect on killing cancer cells, such as vinblastine. The second one is that polysaccharides of some drugs (e.g. purple ganoderma lucidum and evodia rutaecarpa), due to the action on enhancing immunologic function, is very popular as immunotherapy. While there is a limit that polysaccharides almost have no effect on progressive stage and advanced stage of cancer. But because of fewer untoward effects, they can be used as favorable adjuvanticity drugs. The third one is B-type anti-cancer drugs, whose active mechanism is not yet clear. When B-type drug is in high concentration, it can suppress the proliferation of cancer cells but not normal cells. Also it has fewer untoward effects and can be taken for a lone time. But it can neither kill cancer cells nor promote immunologic function. The B-type anti-cancer drug is considered as a kind of new drug.

In nearly a decade, because the writer had the heart issues he rarely goes out and doesn't attend the meeting out of town and other places so that sitting down to do the research work solidly on the detail animal experiment and clinical validation and got many results. With the intensive study, the writer has contacted with a large number of patients monthly, and collected much information that is not recorded in books and literature. And the writer has an intimate knowledge of many patients' epidemiology, clinical symptom, evolution of physical sign and analysis, evaluation and reflection on progress. The writer was sitting down to do a series of the basic research animal experimental work with the Master degree students and the experimental researchers.

II.   Theoretical discussion

1. **Studying the anti-cancer metastasis effect of traditional Chinese medicine from the level of modern molecular biology**

In recent years, at the level of molecular immunopharmacology, looking for anti-cancer, anti-metastatic, anti-recurrence Chinese medicine and new drugs domestic scholars have done a lot of research work.

1. Studying anti-metastatic TCM metastasis from elevated immune function is a complex process that is affected by many factors such as the invasiveness and adhesion of cancer cells, hypercoagulable state and low immune function. Among them, the hypercoagulable state of plasma and low immune function play a major role in cancer metastasis, and **cancer cell retention in the microcirculatory system is a key link in the formation of metastasis.** Therefore, it is necessary to **research and develop traditional Chinese medicines that can improve hypercoagulability, immunosuppression, and microcirculatory disorders at the molecular level.** The XZ-C anti-cancer mixture can significantly inhibit experimental lung metastasis in Lewis lung cancer mice. **The mechanism may be to improve the body's immunity, improve microcirculation, and regulate immune function.** The ephedrine and other blood stasis drugs can enhance immune function, reduce blood viscosity, eliminate microcirculation disorders, thereby reducing the formation and metastasis of cancer thrombus.

2. Research from anti-platelet aggregation

Recent studies on anti-metastatic traditional Chinese medicine have shown that tumor metastasis is closely related to platelets. Cancer cells in the circulation cause host platelet aggregation, which is a key step in the formation of metastasis. After cancer cells enter the blood circulation, they can activate platelets to form cancerous plugs. Some blood-activating and stasis-removing drugs have anticoagulant, anticancer and anti-metastatic effects.Chen Jianmin observed 440 cancer patients and found that 82.7% of the patients had different degrees of high-viscosity, and the treatment with Huayu Decoction Xiaolong Decoction was effective, with an effective rate of 65.2%. Some scholars use Akasaka and Dan to participate in the combination of small-dose chemotherapy drugs, which can significantly reduce lung metastasis of cancer.Cui Wei and other experimental studies have shown that the spatholobus sinensis has a significant inhibitory effect on platelet aggregation, and the depolymerization rate is high. Under the electron microscope, it is observed that the spatholobus sinensis can increase the number of platelets scattered, and is clinically used to counteract the metastasis of tumor thrombus.

3. Study from anti-adhesion therapy

During the metastasis process of anti-metastatic Chinese medicine, cancer cells should adhere to various cells of the host, such as endothelial cells, platelets and lymphocytes, and/or extracellular matrix and basement membrane components, which is one of the important factors for metastasis. Therefore, anti-adhesion therapy may be a new target for anti-metastasis. In recent years it has been found that Salvia can inhibit the adhesion of red blood cells to endothelial cells and platelet aggregation in vitro. It can affect the affinity of tumor cells and host tissues by changing the tumor cell membrane, and has a killing effect on cancer cells. Animal experiments have shown that it can reduce cancer cells into the circulatory system and reduces the adhesion of cancer cells to vascular endothelial cells, reduces the ability to form tumor thrombi, and reduces the chance of cancer cells detaching from the circulatory system.

Dangshen and Atractylodes can significantly inhibit the metastasis of cancer cells in tumor-bearing mice. Qiu Jiaxin et al found that Atractylodes macrocephala has the effect of inhibiting LWeis tumor lung metastasis. The author used BALB/C nude mice as a model to inoculate SGC-7901 human gastric cancer cells 30 days after spleen capsule. The metastasis rate of the control group was 83.33%, and that of the Chinese medicine group was 16.67%. In the clinical aspect, the author randomly divided the patients after radical gastrectomy into two groups, which were divided into Chinese medicine group and chemotherapy group with spleen and qi. One year later, 35.87% of the control group (chemotherapy) had metastasis, while the Chinese medicine group had a metastasis of only 3.33%. After 2 years, the transfer of the Chinese medicine group was 4.76%, while that of the control group was 36.84%.

4. Study from the perspective of regulating cancer cell signaling pathway

The research on anti-cancer and anti-metastatic traditional Chinese medicine signal system has been the frontier of cell biology since the 1980s, that is, it is impossible for various drug molecules in the body to directly enter cells and produce effects, which must be combined with cell-related receptors. Through signal transfer, a second signal system is generated in the cell, and the information is transmitted to the target site to produce an effect. In recent years, the design and development of new anti-cancer and anti-metastatic drugs by regulating cell signaling systems has attracted the attention of scientists.

Haishu (White Dragon Tablet) has significant effects on gastric cancer, lung cancer and bladder cancer. Moreover, it can significantly inhibit the growth of animal solid tumors (liver cancer, lung cancer, cervical cancer); in combination with chemotherapy, it also has the effects of synergistic, attenuating, and enhancing immune function.Liu Jun et al. observed the regulation of sea bream on two sets of CAMP-PKA and DAG-PKC signaling systems in human gastric cancer MGC80-3 cells, as well as the effects on BGC80-3 inhibitory genes in G1 gastric cancer cells and the PKA signaling pathway. Correlation was found to have a significant inhibitory effect on the proliferation of human gastric cancer. From the signal system, the effect of sea bream on MGC80-3 cells was increased by the action of sea lice on MGC80-3 cells for 3 h, and the intracellular cAMP level and PKA activity were increased, while the DAG content and PKc activity were decreased. This is achieved by antagonizing the two sets of signal systems.

2. The exploration of mechanism of action of active ingredients of traditional Chinese medicine on inhibiting or killing cancer cells

1. Traditional Chinese medicine that can inhibit cancer cells and/or kill cancer cells

Experimental studies have proved that some active ingredients of traditional Chinese medicine can inhibit or kill cancer cells. For example, curcumin has a concentration-dependent cytotoxic effect on human gastric adenocarcinoma cell line SGC-7901, which can significantly inhibit the proliferation of SGC_7901 cells, and also has a certain killing effect. Cell lysis necrosis can be seen under electron microscope.

There are also some active ingredients of traditional Chinese medicine that can inhibit cancer cells, such as trichosanthin, elemene, glycyrrhizin, β-carotene, and total ginsenosides.

The extract of Sophora flavescens L. significantly inhibited the proliferation and mitochondrial metabolism of human hepatoma SMMC-7721 cells.

Elemene can significantly inhibit the growth of leukemia HL-60 and K562 cells, block cancer cells from S phase into G2/M phase, and induce apoptosis.

2. Traditional Chinese medicine that can affect the proliferating cells of the cell cycle

Most anticancer Chinese medicines are cell cycle specific drugs. It mainly kills cells in the proliferative phase, especially the S phase and M phase cells are most sensitive to traditional Chinese medicine. In vitro experiments with tanshinone showed that it significantly inhibited the DNA synthesis of cancer cells. Tanshinone acts on the S phase of the cell division cycle, inhibits DNA synthesis, and has a cytotoxic effect.

Another example is that Ginseng polysaccharide can effectively block the synthesis of DNA in S phase cancer cells. Laiyangshen and Gynostemma pentaphyllum mainly act on the G2/M phase of SPC-A-1 cells, blocking cancer cells for mitosis. It can be seen that these drugs affect the proliferation and differentiation of cancer cells by changing the cancer cells 13NA and protein metabolism.

3. Traditional Chinese medicine that can induce apoptosis of cancer cells

With the deepening of genetic research, it has been confirmed that the rapid growth, spread and metastasis of cancer cells are caused by too little cell death and excessive cell proliferation. This degree of disorder results from a decrease or loss of apoptosis. It is necessary to strengthen the study of drug-induced apoptosis in cancer cells. Some traditional Chinese medicine active ingredients can induce apoptosis in cancer cells. For example, trichosanthin has a significant inhibitory effect on mouse melanoma cells and can increase the G0/G1 phase cells of tumor cells, the S phase cells decreased, showing a significant G0/G1 phase arrest. Block cancer cell proliferation and induce apoptosis in cancer cells.

Another example is the anticancer drug paclitaxel extracted from the bark of the natural drug yew, and its cytotoxic effect on cancer cells is related to its induction of apoptosis. The pharmacological and clinical trials of elemene have demonstrated a definite effect on cancer. Flow cytometry confirmed that it blocks cancer cells from entering the G2/M phase from S phase and induces apoptosis.

4. Traditional Chinese medicine that can affect cancer cell genes and inhibit the expression of cancerous cells

The p53 gene is a tumor suppressor gene that inhibits cell proliferation. Wei Xiaolong et al studied the effect of low molecular weight rehmannia polysaccharide (LRPS) on p53 gene expression. It was found that LRPs at the optimal anticancer doses of 20 mg/kg and 40 mg/kg, the expression levels of p53 gene in Lewis lung cancer cells were 1.52 and 1.48, respectively, compared with 0.46 in the control group, indicating that LRP can significantly increase the expression of p53 gene in Lewis lung cancer cells. Conclusion The effect of LRPS on the expression of anti-oncogene p53 is one of the mechanisms of its anti-cancer effect.In another example, icariin can decrease the expression levels of bcl-2 and c-myc genes. Arsenic oxide present in vermiculite and realgar can significantly down-regulate the bcL-2 gene, resulting in a decrease in the bcl-2/bax ratio.

5. Traditional Chinese medicine that can induce differentiation of cancer cells

Tumor cell differentiation therapy is a hot spot in international tumor research, which is characterized by not killing tumor cells and inducing tumor cells to differentiate into normal cells or close to normal cells.In the past 10 years, domestic scholars have begun research on the differentiation of tumor cells induced by traditional Chinese medicine. So far, dozens of Chinese herbal extracts have been found to induce tumor cell differentiation in experiments. Yi Yonglin et al. used ginseng total saponins (GSL) to study the effects of 58 cases of acute non-lymphocytic leukemia, showing that different types of cells have different degrees of differentiation induction. For example, notoginsenoside R1 has a strong induction of differentiation of HL-60 cells (human promyelocytic leukemia cell line) into granulocyte cell lines. The active ingredient alizarin F101 extracted from alfalfa has the effect of inhibiting tumor cell proliferation and activating peritoneal macrophages in mice.

Many experiments have found that there is a certain relationship between effective induction of leukemia cell differentiation and inhibition of its proliferation. Han Rui et al found that cinnamon-like Chinese medicine contains cinnamic acid and its derivatives, and cloning high-transfer lung giant cell carcinoma (PGCL3) cells was treated with cinnamic acid it was found that tumor cells showed a change to normal cells in terms of morphology, proliferation rate, division index, and aggregation reaction. At the same time, the ability of tumor cells to invade and metastasize was significantly reduced. Xu Jianguo et al found that 22 kinds of Chinese herbal medicine water extracts had different degrees of differentiation and differentiation on HL60 cells. The emulsifier of the active ingredient of β-elemene milk turmeric, Qian Jun et al., after 30 μg/ml was used on human lung cancer cells cultured in vitro, found that the growth of lung cancer cells was inhibited, and the effect of the drug was found by flow cytometry analysis for 72 h. After that, the proportion of G0/G1 phase cells in lung cancer increased, and the proportion of S phase decreased. Under light microscopy and electron microscopy, it was observed that the proliferation of cancer cells slowed down, rounded down, microvilli decreased, nuclear ratio decreased, and heterochromatin was observed. The increase suggests that the drug can reverse the phenotype of human lung cancer cells at the level of cell biology and morphology, and induce these cells to differentiate.

Chinese medicine and its active ingredient found in the above studies provides useful ideas and references, and provides new ideas, methods and evaluation criteria for the treatment of cancer by Chinese medicine for mechanism research of the search, development and differentiation induction of tumor differentiation inducers in the future. Traditional Chinese medicine regulates the dysfunction of the body. In the past, it only referred to the adjustment of the function of the viscera, however, yhe traditional Chinese medicine differentiation therapy is to regulate its proliferation and apoptosis and regulate the regulation of its proliferation and differentiation at the cellular level, molecular biological level and gene level. The cancer cells are immature cells with incomplete differentiation, and the Chinese medicine induces differentiation agents to further differentiate them completely. It develops into mature cells and loses malignant features, which is also a kind of "righting" treatment at the cellular level. The standard of efficacy is the emergence of differentiation indicators, the disappearance of malignant features of tumors, and the prolongation of survival of tumor-bearing organisms, but not only the change in the size of the tumor and the emergence of differentiation indicators and the prolongation of survival are the most important.

Tumor differentiation induction therapy is the continuous discovery that the development depends on high-efficiency and low-toxicity differentiation inducers. In this respect, Chinese herbal medicine has great advantages. Because of its rich resources of traditional Chinese medicine, Chinese medicine has a long history. It has accumulated a lot of valuable experience for thousands of years, and it has provided extremely favorable conditions for the development and development of high-efficiency and low-toxic Chinese medicine preparations.

In addition to the above-mentioned traditional Chinese medicine chemical structure, active ingredients and other factors, there are other ideas to consider, such as Interferon (IFN), especially IFN-γ, can induce cancer cell differentiation, and there are many drugs that can induce IFN-γ in vivo.

In short, the treatment of tumor-induced differentiation has been paid more and more attention by scholars at home and abroad, and the research and application prospects of Chinese medicine in this field are broad.

13

Experimental Research and Observation of Its Clinical Curative Effects on Treatment of Malignant Tumor with XZ-C Traditional Chinese Anti-cancer Immune Regulation and Control Medication

In order to look for the traditional herb medicine with actually curative effect and without toxication and adverse reaction, this surgical tumor research institute has screened 200 kinds of Chinese herbal medicines with so-called anticancer reaction recorded on Chinese herbal medicine books for tumor-inhibition reaction on the solid carcinoma in the tumor-bearing animal models one by one in the past 4 years. Through long-term in-vivo tumor-inhibiting animal experiments, we have screened 48 kinds of Chinese herbal medicines with relatively good tumor-inhibition rate that can prolong the survival time, protect the immune organ and obviously improve the immunologic function. According to the clinical conditions, the anticancer medicines screened are combined into 2 compounds including $Z-C_1$ and $Z-C_4$ with better anti-cancer reaction than each single medicine. In the original screening, we carried out the tumor-inhibiting animal experiment for each single medicine and now we further carry out the experimental study on these two groups of compounds for the tumor-inhibiting reaction in the solid tumor of the tumor-bearing rats.

1. Experimental Study on Animal

    1) Materials and Method

    (1) Experimental animal: 260 Kunming clon white rats, half of male and female respectively, weight:$21\pm2g$, 8~10 weeks.

    (2) Cell strains and inoculation: hepatic carcinoma H_{22} cell strains, the fresh tumor bodies from the rats with tumor were prepared into the single cell suspended liquid, after dyeing and counting of the cancer cells (1×10^6/ml), 0.2ml normal saline of cancer cell was subject to subcutaneous vaccination at the front axilla at the right side of each rat.

    (3) Drugs and experimental group: the traditional herb medicines $Z-C_1$ and $Z-C_4$ were entirely developed and prepared by Hubei Branch of China Anti-cancer Research Cooperation

of Chinese Traditional Medicine and Western Medicine, the former was a compound and the latter was a medicinal powder. The chemotherapy control medicine used by the chemotherapy group was cyclophosphane (CTX).

Experimental group: the animals with H_{22} cancer cell transplanted were divided into four groups randomly: ① traditional herb medicine Z-C$_1$ group (90 rats). The rats were subject to gastriclavage once every day after 24h of transplantation of cancer cells, 0.8ml per rat every time, equivalent to 1.4mg of the dried medicinal herbs. ②Traditional herb medicine Z-C$_4$ group (90 rats), as to the dose and gastriclavage method, ditto. ③Chemotherapy group (50 rats), from the next day after transplantation of cancer cells, they were subject to gastriclavage with CTX50mg/kg weight every other day. ④Control group (30 rats), they were subject to gastriclavage with normal saline every day from the next day after transplantation of the cancer cells, 0.8ml/rat.

(4) Observation of indexes: measure the weight of the rats every 3d, measure the diameter of the tumor with vernier caliper, measure the immunologic function and blood picture. Half of each group as Group A, subject to tumor-bearing experiment, regular killing of the rats in batches, separation of tumor and weighing of the tumor and then calculation of tumor-inhabiting rate. The tumor was subject to the pathological section and a few of the specimens were subject to the observation of ultra-structural organization. The rest half of each group as Group B. The tumor-bearing experimental rats were drenched for a long time until they met with natural death. Then the tumor was separated and weighed, the long-term inhibition rate and life elongation rate of the tumor was calculated.

2) Experimental result

(1) The tumor-inhibition effect of Z-C Medicine on Rats bearing hepatic carcinoma H_{22}: in the second week after administration of Z-C$_1$, the tumor-inhibition rate was 40% and the one in the fourth week was 45% and 58% in the sixth week. The tumor-inhibition rate after administration of Z-C$_4$ was 55%, 68% in the fourth week and 70% in the sixth week. (P<0.01) the tumor-inhibiting rate after administration of CTX was 45% in the second week, 45% in the fourth week and 49% in the sixth week (See Fig.1 and 2).

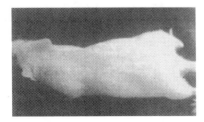
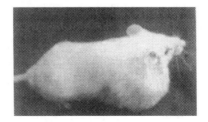

Fig. 1 Z-C1 and Z-C4 therapy group   Fig. 2 Control group

30d after inoculation of hepatic carcinoma H22

30d after inoculation of hepatic carcinoma H_{22}

(2) The effect of Z-C medicine on the survival time of the rats bearing hepatic carcinoma H$_{22}$: the average survival time of Z-C$_1$, Z-C$_4$ and CTX was longer than the one of the normal saline control group (P<0.01); Z-C medicine played a role in obviously prolonging the survival time. Through comparison with the control group, the life elongation rate of Z-C$_1$ group was 85%, the one of Z-C$_4$ group was 200% and the one of CTX group was 9.8%. The rats in Z-C$_1$ and CTX in Group B met with death in 75d. 6 rats bearing carcinoma in Z-C$_4$ survived after seven months.

(3) Both Z-C$_1$ and Z-C$_4$ medicine improved the immunologic function and Z-C$_4$ obviously improved the immunologic function, increased the white blood cells and red blood cells, without any effect on the hepatic function and kidney function and without damage to the hepatic and kidney section. CTX decreased the white blood cells and reduced the immunologic function with the renal damage to the kidney section. The thymus in the control group was obviously atrophic (Fig. 1-4) while the one of Z-C$_1$ and Z-C$_2$ therapy group was not atrophic but a little hypertrophic (Fig.1-3).

Fig. 3 Z-C4 therapy group

The thymus was obviously hypertrophic in 30 days after inoculation of hepatic carcinoma H22

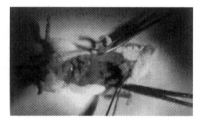

Fig. 4 Control group

The thymus was obviously atrophic in 30 days after inoculation of hepatic carcinoma H22

Fig. 5 Pathological section of the thymus in tumor-bearing control group

HE x 100 cortex atrophia lymphocyte obviously decreased, cortical area formed an empty band of lymphocyte and the sludge appeared in the blood vessel.

Fig. 6 Thymus of Z-C4 control group

HE x 100 the cortex and medulla of the thymus built up and the lymphocyte was highly dense

Pathological section of thymus in the control group: the cortex of the thymus was atrophic, the cells were discrete and the blood vessel met with sludge (Fig. 1-5). The pathological section of the thymus in Z-C_4 therapy group displayed that the cortical area of the thymus built up, the lymphocyte was dense, the epithelium reticulocyte increased and the thymus corpuscles increased (Fig. 1-6).

2. Observation on Clinic Application

1) Clinical information

(1) Hubei Branch of China Anti-cancer Research Cooperation of Chinese Traditional Medicine and Western Medicine, Anti Carcinoma Metastasis and Recurrence Research Office and Shuguang Tumor Specialized Outpatient Department had treated 4, 698 carcinoma patients in Stage III and IV or in metastasis and recurrence with Z-C medicine combined with western medicine from 1994 to Nov. 2002, among which there were 3, 051 men patients and 1,647 women patients. The youngest one was 11 years old and the oldest one was 86 years old, the high invasion age was 40-69 years. All groups of the patients were entirely subject to the diagnosis of pathological histology or definitive diagnosis with ultrasonic B, CT and MRI iconography. According to the staging standard of UICC, all the cases were entirely the patients in medium and advanced stage over Stage III. In this group, there were 1,021 hepatic carcinoma patients, among which there were 694 primary lesion hepatic carcinoma patients and 327 metastatic hepatic carcinoma patients; there were 752 patients suffering from carcinoma of lung, among which there were 699 patients suffering from the primary carcinoma of lung and 53 patients suffering from the metastatic carcinoma of lung; there were 668 gastric carcinoma patients, 624 patients suffering from esophagus cardia carcinoma, 328 patients suffering from rectum carcinoma of anal canal, 442 patients suffering from carcinoma of colon, 368 patients suffering from breast carcinoma, 74 patients suffering from adenocarcinoma of pancreas, 30 patients suffering from carcinoma of bile duct, 43 patients suffering from retroperitoneal tumor, 38 patients suffering from oophoroma, 9 patients suffering from cervical carcinoma, 11 patients suffering from cerebroma, 34 patients suffering from thyroid carcinoma, 38 patients suffering from nasopharyngeal carcinoma, 9 patients suffering from melanoma, 27 patients suffering from kidney carcinoma, 48 patients suffering from carcinoma of urinary bladder, 13 patients suffering from leukemia, 47 patients suffering from metastasis of supraclavicular lymph nodes, 35 patients suffering various fleshy tumors and 39 patients suffering from other malignancies.

(2) Medicine and medication: the treatment aims to support healthy energy to eliminate evils, soften and resolve the hard mass and supplement qi and blood. Z-C_1 is the compound, 150ml to be taken on the daily basis, Z-C_4 is powder, 10g to be taken on the daily basis. According to the analysis and differentiation of the diseases, anti-cancer powder shall be taken orally and the anti-cancer apocatastasis paste shall be applied externally for the solid tumor or the metastatic tumor. In case of being in pain, anti-cancer aponic paste shall be

applied externally. Icterus removal soup or dropsy removal soup shall be taken orally for the patients suffering from icterrus and the ascites.

(3) Therapeutic evaluation: it pays attention to the short-term curative effect and iconography indexes as well as the survival time of long-term curative effect, quality of life and immunologic indexes. Attention shall be paid to the changes in subjective signs in administration of drugs. It will be effective when the subjective signs are improved and last over one month; otherwise, it will be ineffective. As to the quality of life (Karnofsky Performance Status), it will be effective when it is improved and lasts over one month, otherwise, it will be ineffective. As to the evaluation standard of the curative effect of solid tumor, it can be divided into four levels according to the changes in size of tumor: Level I: disappearance of tumor; Level II: tumor reduces 1/2; Level III: softening of tumor; Level IV: no change or enlargement of level tumor.

2) Curative results

(1) The symptom was improved, the quality of life was improved, the survival time was prolonged: among the 4,277 carcinoma patients in medium and advanced stage who took Z-C medicine with the return visit over 3 months, the case history had the specific observation record of the curative effect, see Table 1-1. It improved the quality of life of the patients in an all-round way, see Table 1-2.

Table 1-1 General information about 4,277 patients suffering from recurrence and metastasis

		Hepatic carcinoma	Carcinoma of lung	Gastric carcinoma	Esophagus cardia carcinoma	Rectum carcinoma of anal canal	Carcinoma of colon	Breast carcinoma	adenocarcinoma of pancreas
No. of cases		1 021	752	668	624	328	442	368	74
Male: female		4:1	4.4:1	2.25:1	3.1:1	1:1	2.1:1	Female	3.2:1
Focus	Primary	694 (68.6%)	699 (93.9%)						
	Metastasis	327 (31.2%)	53 (6.1%)						
Usual metastasis part in this group		Metastatic lung (2) From the stomach (31.2%)	Metastasis of supraclavicular lymph nodes (11.6%)	Metastatic lever (23.8%) Lung metastasis (3%)	Upper metastasis of compact bone (13.1%)	Reoccurrence rate (14.8%)	Metastatic lever (16.0%)	Metastasis of supraclavicular lymph nodes (17.5%)	Metastatic lever (11.7%)
		From esophagus cardia (19.5%) From recta (31.2%)	Brain metastasis (3.1%) Bone metastasis (4.6%)	Metastasis of peritoneum (29.1%) Upper metastasis of compact bone (6.1%)	Metastatic lever (8.3%)	Metastatic lever (7.0%)	Metastasis of peritoneum (6.0%)	Metastasis of axillary lymph nodes (15.0%) Bone metastasis (5.0%)	Rear metastasis of peritoneum (39.1%)

Age	high invasion (year) %	30~39 (76.2)	50~69 (71.6)	40~49 (73.4)	40~69 (80.4)	40~49 (75.2)	30~69 (88.0)	40~59 (65.9)	40~59 (70.0)
	Oldest (year) %	11	20	17	30	27	27	29	34
	Youngest (year) %	86	80	77	77	78	76	80	68

Table 1-2 Observation of curative effect on 4 277 patients: fully improving the quality of life of the carcinoma patients in medium and advanced stage

Improvement	Vigor	Appetite	Reinforcement of physical force	Improvement in generalized case	Increase of body weight	Improvement of sleep	The restriction of improvement activity and capability released activity	self servicing normal walking	Resumption of work Engaged in light work
No. of cases	4071	3986	2450	479	2938	1005	1038	3220	479
(%)	95.2	93.2	57.3	11.2	68.7	23.5	24.3	75.3	11.2

In this group, all of them were the patients in medium and advanced stage. After taking the medicine, their symptoms were improved to different extents with the effective rate of 93.2%. With respect to the improvement of the quality of life (as per Karnofsky Performance Status), it rose to 80 scores on average after administration from 50 on average before administration; the patients in this group met with the different metastasis and dysfunction of the organs about Stage III. It was reported by the previous statistic information that the mesoposition survival time of this kind of patients was about 6 months. The longest time among this group of the cases reached up to 11 years; another patient suffering from hepatic carcinoma had taken Z-C medicine for ten years and a half; two patients suffering from hepatic carcinoma met with frequency encountered carcinomatous lesion in the left and right liver and it entirely subsided through secondary CT reexamination after the patient took Z-C medicine for half a year and the state of the disease had been stable over half a year. One patient suffering from double-kidney carcinoma met with the widespread metastasis of abdominal cavity after removal of one kidney, after taking Z-C medicine, he was entirely recovered and began to work again. 3 patients suffering from carcinoma of lung, with the lung not removed through explaraton, had taken Z-C medicine over three years and a half. 2 patients suffering from gastric remnant carcinoma had taken Z-C medicine for 8 years. 3 patients suffering from reoccurrence of rectal carcinoma had taken Z-C medicine for 3 years. 1 patient suffering from metastatic liver and rib of the mastocarcinoma had taken Z-C medicine for 8 years. 1 patient suffering from the recurrent bladder carcinoma after operation of renal carcinoma had not met with the carcinoma for 9 years and a half after taking Z-C medicine. All of these patients were the ones in the medium and advanced stage that could not be operated once more or treated with radiotherapy or chemotherapy. They only took Z-C medicine without other medicines for treatment. Up to today, they are reexamined and get the medicine at the out-patient department every month. Through taking the medicine for a long time, the state of the disease is controlled in the stable state to make the organism and the tumor in balanced state for a relatively long time and get a relatively good survival with tumor, in this way, the symptoms of the patients are improved, the quality of life is improved and the survival time is prolonged.

(2) As to 84 patients suffering from solid tumor and 56 patients suffering from enlargement of upper lymph node of metastatic compact bone, after taking Z-C series medicines orally and applying Z-C3 anti-cancer apocatastasis paste, they met with good curative effects, see table 1-3.

Table 1-3 Changes of 84 patients suffering from solid tumor and 56 patients suffering from metastatic mode after applying Z-C paste externally

	Solid tumor				Enlargement of upper lymph node of metastatic compact bone			
	Disappearance	Shrinkage 1/2	Softening	No change	Disappearance	Shrinkage 1/2	Softening	No change
No. of cases	12	28	32	12	12	22	14	8
(%)	14.2	33.3	38.0	14.2	21.4	39.2	25.0	14.2
Total effective rate (%)	85.7				85.7			

(3) 298 patients suffering from carcinoma pain obtained the obvious pain alleviation effects after taking Z-C medicine orally and applying Z-C anti-cancer apocatastasis paste externally, see Table 1-4.

Clinical menifetation	Pain			
	Light alleviation	Obvious alleviation	Disappearance	Avoidance
No of cases	52	139	93	14
(%)	17.3	46.8	31.2	4.7
Total effective rate (%)	95.3			

3. Discussion about Z-C Medicine Experiment and Clinic Curative Effect

1) Tumor-inhibition effect of Z-C$_{1-4}$ Medicine on hepatic carcinoma H$_{22}$ rats bearing tumor

It was found that after the medicine was taken to H$_{22}$ tumor-bearing rats for two weeks, four weeks and six weeks, the tumor inhibition rate increased with the prolongation of the administration time, the tumor inhibition rate of Z-C$_4$ in the 6th week reached up to 70%. Through two repeated experiments in succession, the results were stable, which indicated that the tumor-inhibition effect of Chinese herb medicine was slow and it would increase gradually, that is to say, the tumor-inhibition effect was of positive correlation to the accumulated dosage of Chinese herb medicine.

The effect on the survival time of hepatic carcinoma H_{22} tumor-bearing rats from Z-C_1 and Z-C_4 medicine: it was proven by the experimental results that Z-C_1 and Z-C_4 medicine could obviously prolong the survival time of the tumor-bearing rats, especially Z-C_4, it could prolong the survival time as long as 200%, more than that, Z-C_4 could remarkably improve the immunologic function of the organism, protect the immune organ and the bone marrow, alleviate the toxic action and side effect of the radiotherapy and chemotherapy medicines. Furthermore, no toxic action or side effect had been found in the past 12 months after the rats took the medicine. The above-mentioned experimental study offered the beneficial basis to the clinical application.

2) Clinical curative effect

Based on the experimental study, it had been applied to various clinical carcinomas, most of the patients were the ones over Stage III and IV, namely: the ones suffering from the cancer of late stage that could not be removed with exploratory operation; the ones with the exploratory operation without operation indication; the ones meeting with metastasis or reoccurrence in short term or long term after operation of the carcinoma; the ones suffering from hepatic metastasis, lung metastasis or brain metastasis or with cancerous pleural effusion or cancerous ascites in late stage; the ones suffering from various carcinomas conservative removal operation with the exploratory operation only for the anastomosis of intestines and stomach or colostomy but not for removal and the ones not suitable for the operation, chemotherapy and radiotherapy and so on. Through over 10 years' clinical application and systematic observation, Z-C_1 and Z-C_4 medicine had obtained remarkable curative effect and no toxic action and side effect had been found after long-term administration. It had been proven by the clinical observation that Z-C_1 and Z-C_4 medicine could improve the survival quality of the carcinoma patients in medium and late stage in an all-round way, improve the whole immunity, control the hyperplasia of the cancer cells, consolidate and enhance the long-term curative effect. The oral-taken and external-applied Z-C medicine had good curative effect in softening and shrinking body surface metastatic tumor. With the assistance of intervention or treatment with cannula spray pump for medicine, it could protect liver, kidney and bone marrow hemopoietic system and the immune organ and improve the immune function.

3) Good pain alleviation effect of Z-C anti-cancer pain alleviation paste

Pain is the relatively remarkable and painful symptom of the carcinoma patients in late stage, the common pain reliever had no remarkable effect on carcinoma pain, the stupefacient pain reliever had the addiction and dependence, Z-C anti-cancer pain alleviation paste had strong pain alleviation effect with a long maintenance time. It was proven through 298 cases of clinical verification that the effective rate was 78.0%, the total effective rate was 95.3%, after repeated application, there were no toxic action or side effect, without addiction. The paid alleviation effect was stable and it was an effective therapeutic method for the carcinoma patients to get rid of the pain and improve the quality of life.

Through experimental research and clinical validation, our experience is: Chinese medicine with Chinese characteristics has its unique advantage in cancer treatment, such as a strong overall concept, conditioning prominent role, mild side effects, can relieve pain, relieve symptoms, and significantly improved quality of life of patients, can mobilize the body's immune function and overall disease resistance, improve the therapeutic effect.

4. The research on cytokine induction factors of XZ-C anticancer immune regulation and control medication

1) XZ-C_4 induces endogenous cytokines

(1) Through the experiments: XZ-C_4 has many immune strengthening functions and has closely relationship to the induced endogenous cytokines
(2) XZ-C_4 can recover the reduction of the white blood cells, granulation cells and platelets.
(3) XZ-C_4 can have the direct function on GM-CSF production from granulation cell (GM) through IL-1β, also increase TNF, IFN etc all of kind of the cell factors, which are possible the indirect function.
(4) XZ-C_4 can increase the Th1 cell factors, which were decrease in the cancer patients. There are the curative effects on the anemia and the white blood cells decrease due to the chemotherapy.
(5) The experiment analysis showed that XZ-C_4 not only protects the bone marrow function, but also has direct function on the tumor cell division.

In brief, XZ-C_4 can induce the tumor division and natural death through the autocrine which produce all of kind of factors. The autocrine is the secretory things from the host to affect the host's function. XZ-C_4 probably will become the induction therapy to the tumor division in the future.

2) XZ-C_4 inhibiting cancer development and metastasis

The malignant development is defined as tumor cells accepting invasion and metastasis characters during the proliferation. Cancer research need to have good repeated animal models. Then the good repeated animal model was made from the mice fibrosis cancernoma QR-32. QR-32 cannot proliferate after inoculation in the skin, and will completely disappear; there were no metastasis lump after injecting into the vein. However, if QR-32 was injected with Gelatin sponge together under the skin in the mice, QR-32 will become the proliferating tumor cells QRSP.

In vitro culturing QRSP and then transfer into another mice, even if there is no foreign thing, the tumors will grow such as the lung metastasis will happen after injection in the vein.

XZ-C_4 was used in the animal models to search the effects of the tumor development. To divide this animal models into two steps: the process from QR-32 to QRSP(early progress) and from the QRSP to tumor(later progress). After using XZ-C$_4$, the tumor development will be inhibited in these two models, especially the former will be inhibited significantly. And this has relationship with the dose of the medication.

On the survival experiment the animal models of the inoculation of the QR-32 AND Gelatin sponge died during 65 days, however in XZ-C group the mice survival rate for 150 days was 30%. XZ-C$_4$ can increase the immune effects and reduce the side effects of other anticancer medication.

This research proved that XZ-C$_4$ has inhibition of the cancer progression function and inhibit cancer invasion and metastasis.

3) Z-C1+Z-C4 anti-cancer immune regulation medication

Z-C1+Z-C4 anti-cancer immune regulation medication has the following characteristics:

A. An overall improvement in the quality of life of patients with advanced cancer
B. Protect Thymus and increase immune function;
C. Nurse bone morrow and blood and increase immune function
D. Enhance physical fitness, reduce pain and improve physical strength
E. Enhance therapeutic effect and reduce the side effects of chemotherapy

5. Z-C Medication is the Modern Production of Traditional Herb Medication

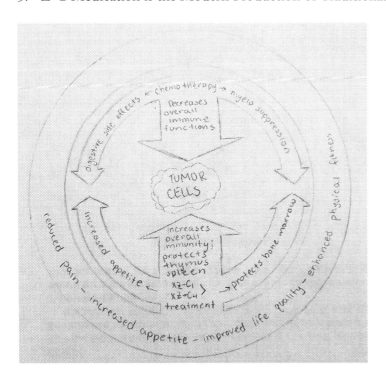

Fig. The characterics of XZ-C immune regulation and control anti-cancer medications

XZ-C immunomodulation anticancer Chinese medicine is not an experience prescription, nor is it an old Chinese medicine practice prescription, but it is the scientific research results of the combination of Chinese and Western medicine and the modernization of traditional Chinese medicine are combined with modern medical methods, experimental tumor research methods and modern pharmacological and pharmacodynamic research methods. After 7 years of more than 4,000 cancer-bearing animal models, 200 commonly used anti-cancer Chinese herbal medicines were screened in animal experiments in batches, and screened for tumor inhibition rates in vitro and in tumor-bearing animals.

48 kinds of traditional Chinese medicines with anti-cancer effects were screened out. Then it was made as these 48 kinds of natural medicines into XZ-C1-10.

According to the respiratory system, digestive system, urinary system, gynecology, endocrine system, the cancer animal models of liver cancer, stomach cancer, colon cancer, breast cancer, bladder cancer and lung cancer were made and the immunological experiments and toxicological experiments in tumor-bearing animals were done, then all of them were made into a series of immune regulate and control anticancer Chinese medicine XZ-C1, XZ-C2, XZ-C3, XZ-C4, XZ-C5, XZ-C6, XZ-C7, XZ-C8 and others.

The physical basis for the traditional prescription to exert its unique therapeutic effect in clinical practice is its chemical composition. Changes in the quality and quantity of chemical constituents directly affects the clinical efficacy of the prescription. Therefore, only the changes in the quality and quantity of chemical components in the formula are studied to find out the main active ingredients of the preparation and to Explore the mystery of its unique efficacy from the perspective of molecular immunology, then it can make the research of traditional prescriptions to a new level. The preparation of XZ-C immunomodulatory Chinese medicine is the innovation and reform of traditional Chinese medicine preparation. It is not a mixed decoction of the chemical, but it is the granule concentrate or powder of each drug and the raw medicine for each of the medicines remains the original ingredient, pharmacological action, molecular weight, structural formula which made with modern scientific methods. It is not a combination, keeping the original ingredients and functions of each flavor unchanged. It is easy to evaluate and affirm the role and efficacy of the drug.

14

BRM-like effect and efficacy of XZ-C immunomodulation anticancer Chinese medication

I.   First, the biological reaction regulation (BRM) theory

In 1982, Oldham founded the biological response modifier (BRM), or BRM theory. On this basis, in 1984, the fourth modality of cancer treatment, biotherapy, was proposed.

According to the BRM theory, under normal circumstances, the tumor and the body's defenses are in a dynamic equilibrium, and the occurrence and even invasion and metastasis of the tumor are completely caused by the imbalance of this dynamic balance. If the state of the disorder has been artificially adjusted to the normal level, it can control the growth of the tumor and cause it to subside.

Specifically, BRM includes the following anti-tumor mechanisms:

1. Promote the enhancement of the effect of the host defense mechanism, or reduce the immune inhibition of the tumor-bearing host, in order to achieve the immune response to cancer.
2. The natural or recombinant bioactive substance is administered to enhance the defense mechanism of the host.
3. Modification of tumor cells induces a strong host response.
4. Promote the differentiation and maturation of tumor leopard cells and normalize them.
5. to reduce the toxicity of cancer chemotherapy, radiotherapy, and enhance the tolerance of the host.

Biotherapeutic treatment is to modulate this biological response by supplementing, inducing or activating, in vitro, a biologically active cell (or) factor of cytotoxic activity of the inherent BRM system. The other three treatment modes of biotherapy different treatments, namely surgery, radiation therapy and chemotherapy, aim to directly attack the tumor.

The scope of biotherapeutics clearly exceeds the traditional concept of immunotherapy because the dynamic balance between the body and the tumor is not limited to immune responses, but also involves various regulatory genes and cytokines involved in tumor proliferation.

Tumor biotherapy mainly includes:

1. adoptive infusion of immunocompetent cells.
2. Lymphokine/cytokine production and application.
3. specific autoimmune, including the application of tumor vaccine, monoclonal antibody and its cross-linking.

The cellular and humoral factors of the body's immune system are in delicate adjustments. In the case of its imbalance, the body's response or response ability will be significantly affected. The use of biological response modifiers is to restore the balance of the body state to normal balance, in order to achieve the purpose of prevention and treatment of cancer.

The biological response modifier regulates the immune function of the body and restores the function of the suppressed immune system. The mechanism of action of these drugs is to exert their regulatory functions by activating the body's immune system. It is known as a microbial and plant source. Previously referred to as an immunopotentiator, immunostimulant or immunomodulator, it is now collectively named Bioreactive Conditioner (BRM).

In recent years, some drugs with BRM-like effects have been discovered from traditional Chinese medicine resources, and have achieved gratifying effects in experimental research and clinical applications.

II.   Second, biological response modifier

1. Cytokines

It is produced by immune effector cells and related cells and is an important biologically active cell regulatory protein that plays an important role in mediating multiple immune responses in the body.

According to its biological inclusion, it can be divided into:

(1) Interleukin:

IL-2 is an immune cell-interacting molecule that promotes the activation of T and B cells and activates killer cells such as N K cells.

(2) Interferon (IFN)

There are three kinds of IFN-a, IFN-γ, and IFN-ß, which are a group of glycoprotein molecules.

(3) Colony stimulating factor (CSF) is a class of factors that stimulate the growth and differentiation of various hematopoietic stem cells. Divided into multi-directional CSF, granulocyte-macrophage CSF (GM-CSF), macrophage CSF (M-CSF) and granulocyte CSF (G-CSF).

(4) Tumor necrosis factor (TNF)

2. Adoptive transfer of immune cells

So far, there are 4 kinds of immune living cells for tumor treatment:

(1) lymphokine killer cells (LAK),
(2) tumor infiltrating lymphocytes (TIL),
(3) PWH-LAK and OKT3-LAK:

 PB or TIL stimulated by P. sinensis (PWH) or solidified anti-CD3 antibody (OKT3), which can increase the proliferative activity of LAN

(4) CD8+ CTL cells that recognize MHC class I tumor antigens have strong tumor killing activity.

3. tumor molecular vaccine

At present, the research of tumor vaccine mainly includes: a unique vaccine against human tumor monoclonal antibody, which can simulate the tumor to stimulate the body to produce an anti-tumor response.

4. natural botanical Chinese medicine with BRM-like effect

XZ-C immunomodules anticancer Chinese medicine has the function and efficacy of BRM-like.

III. Third, the mechanism of action of biological response modifiers

BRM has the effect of modulating host immune response to tumors and killing tumor cells. Its mechanism of action mainly shows the following five aspects:

1. It can directly regulate the growth and differentiation of cancer cells, and regulate the growth and differentiation.
2. It can enhance the sensitivity of cancer cells to the anti-cancer mechanism of the machine, and is conducive to killing cancer cells.
3. acts on tumor blood vessels, affecting the nutrition and blood supply of the tumor, leading to tumor necrosis, while normal tissues are not affected by this damage.
4. Stimulate the host's anti-tumor immune response.
5. Stimulate hematopoietic function, promote the recovery of myelosuppression, and enhance tolerance to tumor treatment damage.

BRM can enhance the body's immune response and strengthen the body's tumor immune surveillance. The greatest effect occurs in patients with particularly small tumors, when patients with sudden changes in cells or tumors, or patients with residual tumors or early tumors.

Immunotherapy should be one of the comprehensive treatments for the treatment of malignant tumors. Some people think that immunotherapy can only deal with cancer cells below 105. If cancer cells have formed obvious tumors, immunotherapy can only limit their growth.

Despite the great development of immunotherapy, it has attracted the attention of the world, but the efficacy of tumor immunotherapy is still different. It is considered to be a work worthy of intensive research. The problems are:

(1) The treatment of large tumors is difficult to work, and can only be used as an auxiliary measure for surgery, chemotherapy and radiotherapy.

(2) Certain tumor antigens only show individual specificity, so preparation of anti-idiotypic antibodies is difficult.

Several studies have shown that:

Anti-tumor therapy does not require absolute specificity. Therefore, even if the tumor does not have a specific antigen, immunotherapy of the tumor is still desirable. The concentration of tumor-associated antigens on malignant cells is much higher than that of normal cells, and these differences are sufficient to make these antigens an effective target. Moreover, since tumor patients mostly have low immune function, increased immunosuppressive factors in the body, and decreased production of IL-2, TNF and IFN, it is necessary to enhance the immune function of patients.

In the above situation, how should we take countermeasures? Because cancer patients have low immune function, we should try to improve the immunity of patients. Due to the increase of immunosuppressive factors in tumor patients, we should deal with and reduce the production of IL-2, TNF and IFN in tumor patients. We should try to activate the increase of these cytokines.

In order to further improve the effectiveness of immunotherapy, it is necessary to further explore the best combination of how to use the existing treatment.

IV. Overview of the research on BRM-like immunomodulation anticancer Chinese medicine

After 7 years of experimental research and 34 years of clinical validation, XZ-C immunomodulation anticancer Chinese medicine has shown its BRM-like effect and efficacy, and is a drug with similar BRM-like effects from the screening of traditional Chinese medicine resources.

XZ-C immunomodulatory anticancer Chinese medicine was experimentally screened from 200 Chinese herbal medicines by the laboratory of Professor XU ZE-China (XZ-C). The cancer cells were cultured in vitro and 200 Chinese herbal medicines were screened in vitro. Screening and observing the direct damage of each drug to cultured tuberculosis cancer cells, and comparing the tumor inhibition rate with the chemotherapy drug CTX and normal cells cultured in vitro.

Results: A batch of drugs with a certain tumor inhibition rate for cancer cell proliferation were selected.Then, the tumor-bearing animal model was further fabricated, and the experimental study on the in vivo anti-tumor rate screening of the tumor-bearing animal model was carried out on 200 kinds of Chinese herbal medicines. The scientific, objective and rigorous experimental screening, analysis and evaluation were carried out. The results of the experiment proved that only 48 kinds of tumors have a good tumor inhibition rate, and the other 152 kinds of Chinese herbal medicines are common Chinese medicines for treating traditional Chinese medicine. After the tumor inhibition rate in this group of tumor-bearing tumors, the results showed no anti-cancer effect or the effect of tumor inhibition rate is minimal.

Our experimental screening work is mainly the in vivo anti-tumor experiment of the tumor-bearing animal model. One experimental group of traditional Chinese medicine observes the chronic experiment in vivo for 3 months, and after screening 48 effective anti-cancer Chinese herbal medicines, it will be every 2 flavors, 3 flavors. The anti-tumor experiment of tumor-bearing animals is carried out with raw medicine. We have also found that the anti-tumor test of single-flavor crude drug is not as good as the anti-tumor effect of the compound anti-tumor experiment with optimized combination of several kinds of raw drugs. It seems that the single-flavored crude drug only has an effect on the inhibition of tumor growth, and the compound of the multi-flavored drug-optimized combination It not only inhibits the growth of tumor-bearing mice, but also regulates the body, enhances physical strength, boosts immunity, promotes the production of tumor suppressor cytokines, protects normal cells, and promotes anti-tumor cytokines. Our experimental screening work is mainly the in vivo anti-tumor experiment of the tumor-bearing animal model. One experimental group of traditional Chinese medicine observes the chronic experiment in vivo for 3 months, and after screening 48 effective anti-cancer Chinese herbal medicines, it will be every 2 flavors, 3 flavors. The anti-tumor experiment of tumor-bearing animals is carried out with raw medicine.

We have also found that the anti-tumor test of single-flavor crude drug is not as good as the anti-tumor effect of the compound anti-tumor experiment with optimized combination of several kinds of raw drugs. It seems that the single-flavored crude drug only has an effect on the inhibition of tumor growth, and the compound of the multi-flavored drug-optimized combination It not only inhibits the growth of tumor-bearing mice, but also regulates the body, enhances physical strength, boosts immunity, promotes the production of tumor suppressor cytokines, protects normal cells, and promotes anti-tumor cytokines.

Our laboratory is based on the cancer inhibition screening test for the single-flavor Chinese medication in the early stage of 4 years screening in vitro and in the tumor-bearing animal model in vivo tumor inhibition experiment screening, and then experimentally optimized combination, and then after the experiment, it reconstitutes the compound of XZ-C1-10 immunoregulation against cancer, anti-metastasis and anti-recurrence. Finally, clinical validation is performed. Since 1992, we have formed a collaborative group for clinical validation. So far, after 11 years, the clinical verification system of more than 12,000 patients with various pains in the oncology clinic has achieved stable, improved, improved symptoms, improved quality of life, and significantly prolonged survival. Many patients with metastases stabilized the lesions without further spread and metastasis. Some patients were unable to receive chemotherapy after leukopenia and other reasons. After taking the drug, the metastasis was controlled and no metastasis was achieved. Both have achieved good results.

V.   BRM-like effects and efficacy of XZ-C immunomodulation anticancer
Chinese medicine

Biological Response Regulation (BRM) was first described by Oldham in 1982 with the concept of BRM. Its significance is the ability to regulate the body's response or response to external "attacks" through biological response agents.

The cellular and humoral factors of the body's immune system are in delicate regulation. Under the unbalanced condition, the body's response or response ability will be significantly affected. The use of biological response modifiers is to restore the balance of the body state to normal balance, in order to achieve disease prevention.

BRM opened a new field of cancer biotherapy. At present, BRM is widely regarded as the fourth mode of cancer treatment by the medical community. The biological response modifier regulates the immune function of the body and restores the function of the suppressed immune system. The mechanism of action of these drugs is multifaceted, but regardless of the mechanism, it activates the regulatory function by activating the body's immune system.

Biological response modifiers, mostly microbial and plant sources, formerly known as immunostimulants, or immunomodulators, immune strengthenor, immune stimulator, immune exciting factors or immune regulation are now collectively named biological response modifiers or modifiers (BRM).

In the laboratory, the author screened the XZ-C immunomodulatory anti-cancer and anti-metastasis Chinese medicine which has a good tumor inhibition rate in the laboratory. It has improved immunity, protects the central immune organ thymus, improves cellular immunity, and protects the thymus tissue function, improve immunity, protect bone marrow blood function, increase the number of red blood cells and white blood cells, activate immune fine-holding factors, and improve immune surveillance in blood. The main pharmacological action of XZ-C immune regulation anti-cancer Chinese medicine is anti-cancer and increase immune function.

After 4 years of animal experiments, this group was screened out 48 kinds of drugs with high tumor inhibition rate, and detected 26 of them to enhance phagocytosis function; or enhance cellular immunity; or enhance body fluids immune function; or increase thymus weight; or promote bone cell proliferation; or enhance T cell function; or enhance LAX cell activity; or enhance interferon IFN activity; or enhance TNF activity; or enhance CSF colony stimulating factor; inhibiting coagulation and antithrombotic; or anti-tumor, anti-metastasis; or scavenging free radicals.

The anti-cancer mechanism of the above XZ-C immunomodulation anticancer traditional Chinese medicine is:

1. Activate the body's immune cell system, promote the enhancement of the host defense mechanism, and achieve the immune response to pain.
2. Activate the immune cytokine system of the body's anti-cancer mechanism, enhance the host's immune defense mechanism and improve the immune surveillance of the immune cells of the body's blood circulation system.

3. Protect Thymus and Enhance Immune function, protect the marrow from blood, protect the bone marrow from blood, stimulate the bone to hematopoietic function; promote the recovery of bone marrow suppression, increase white blood cells, red blood cells, etc.

4. It can alleviate the side effects of radiotherapy and chemotherapy and enhance the tolerance of the host.

5. The progression of cancer is caused by the imbalance between the biological characteristics of cancer cells and the body's ability to restrict cancer. The XZ-C immunomodulatory effect is to improve the degree of freedom and restore balance.

6. It can directly regulate the growth and differentiation of tumor cells, and regulate the growth and differentiation.

7. It can increase the weight of the thymus and make the thymus not progressively atrophy. As the cancer progresses, the foot glands undergo progressive atrophy.

8. It stimulates the host's anti-tumor immune response, enhances the body's ability to fight cancer, and strengthens the sensitivity of cancer cells to the body's anti-cancer mechanism, which is conducive to the killing of cancer cells on the way to metastasis.

XZ-C immunomodulation Chinese medicine treatment of tumors can enable the host to produce a strong immune response to cancer cells and achieve the purpose of treating cancer. XZ-C immunomodulation anti-pain Chinese medicine can cause the following immunological reactions in the host; enhance the regulation or restore the host's immune response to the tumor; stimulate the body's inherent immune function, activate the host's immune defense system; restore immune function. As mentioned above, the mechanism of action of XZ-C immunomodulation anticancer Chinese medicine is basically similar to that of BRM, and the clinical use also has the same therapeutic effect as BRM.

VI. Clinical application principles and adaptation range of XZ-C immunomodulation anticancer Chinese medicine

1. Application principle of XZ-C immunomodulation anticancer Chinese medicine

   BRM and BRM-like XZ-C immunomodulation anticancer Chinese medicine can enhance the body's immune response. It can strengthen the body's tumor immune surveillance, and it is better when the cells are mutated or the tumor is very small. Through surgery or radiation therapy, drug treatment works best when the tumor is minimized.

   For those who have lost the opportunity to operate, have poor physical fitness, can not tolerate radiotherapy and chemotherapy, immunotherapy has a certain effect, can alleviate symptoms and prolong survival time.

   After radical resection of the tumor, in order to reduce recurrence and metastasis, XZ-C immunomodulation can be used to treat traditional Chinese medicine. After surgical resection of large tumors, it is also feasible to eliminate cancer cells that may remain and distant cancer cells, XZ-C immune regulation Chinese medicine treatment can be used.

If the tumor cannot be removed, radiotherapy or chemotherapy can be used first to kill the tumor cells in a large amount, so that the tumor burden in the body is reduced, and then XZ-C immunomodulation is used to treat the Chinese medicine.

2. Clinical observation and response range of XZ-C immunomodulation anticancer Chinese medicine

    (1) Post-cancer metastasis:

    Restore and improve postoperative immunity, improve postoperative quality of life, kill residual cancer cells, prevent metastasis, inhibit cancer cell proliferation, prevent recurrence, consolidate and enhance long-term efficacy. Adaptation:

    1 after various radical cancer surgery; 2 after palliative resection of various cancers; 3 exploration can not be removed after advanced cancer surgery; 4 can only be used for gastrointestinal anastomosis or colostomy; 5 advanced tumor can not Excision, loss of surgical indications; 6 tumor resection + intubation pump after surgery.

    (2) Comprehensively improve the quality of life of patients with advanced cancer, prolong survival, inhibit mitosis of cancer cells, control the proliferation of cancer cells, and improve overall immunity, mainly for anti-proliferation.

    Adaptation range: 1 recent or long-term metastasis after various pains, or recurrence; 2 liver metastases of various advanced cancers, lung metastasis, brain metastasis, or with cancerous pleural effusion, cancerous ascites.

    (3) Relieve cancer pain: Oral or external application of XZ-C medicine for the treatment of various stagnation advanced intractable pain and softening, reducing body surface metastasis:

    (4) In combination with interventional therapy or fistula pump treatment, protect liver, 'kidney, bone marrow hematopoietic system and immune organs such as Thymus, improve immunity, improve overall immune status after injection treatment, maintain, consolidate and enhance injection The efficacy of intermittent and long-term, prevent metastasis, prevent spread, prevent recurrence, comprehensively improve and improve the survival quality of patients with liver cancer or other intubation treatment, and prolong survival.

    (5) with radiotherapy and chemotherapy:

    It can reduce toxic and side effects, enhance the therapeutic effect, protect the liver, kidney, bone marrow hematopoietic system and immune organs, improve immune function, and raise white blood cells.

(6) XZ-C immunomodulation anticancer traditional Chinese medicine combined with traditional Chinese medicine decoction:

Such as the combination of anti-cancer Shugan Xiaoshui Decoction for the treatment of liver cancer and ascites or abdominal abdomen to transfer cancerous ascites;

Combined with Xuehuang Decoction for the treatment of liver cancer and jaundice;

Combined with Jiangfu Zhunyin Decoction for the treatment of liver cancer with high transaminase and HbsAg positive components.

Combined with Shengxue Decoction to treat leukopenia caused by chemotherapy.

3. The timing of application of XZ-C immunomodulation anticancer Chinese medicine

Most cancer patients have low immune function. After diagnosis, they should be treated. The three major treatments of surgery, radiotherapy and chemotherapy may promote the patient's immune function, which will reduce the patient's endurance to surgery or chemotherapy and radiotherapy. And reduce the immune surveillance within the immune system of the patient's body. Therefore, immunotherapy should be started during surgery or during radiotherapy or chemotherapy. XZ-C immunomodulatory Chinese medicine is an oral drug, as long as the patient can eat orally take XZ-C Chinese medicine. It is usually taken 1-2 weeks after surgery. XZ-C immunomodulation of traditional Chinese medicine for a period of time after radiotherapy, pre-chemotherapy and radiotherapy and chemotherapy, and after completion of chemotherapy and chemotherapy, may be beneficial to reduce or reduce recurrence and metastasis. This is beneficial to reduce the side effects of radiotherapy and chemotherapy, prevent chemotherapy from causing low immune function and improve skin protection; promote bone marrow blood production and protect the marrow from blood; activate the body's immune cell system and immune cytokine system to improve immune surveillance, which is beneficial to Prevent recurrence and metastasis.

15

Typical cases of treatment for malignant tumor by XZ-C traditional Chinese anticancer medicine through immunological regulation and control

There are a variety of following of typical cases which Z-C anticancer immune regulation, anti-metastatic therapy were applied in our Cancer Research and the National Cooperative Group Hubei

一. **The typical cases of inoperable, nor radiotherapy and chemotherapy, simply taking Z-C immunomodulatory anticancer medicine treatment**

Case 1 Mr. Liu, male, 68year-old, Changzhou, officer, Medical record number:8701735
Diagnosis: the central lung cancer on the right upper of the lung with the metastasis

Disease courses and treatment: in Octocber 1998 he coughed two weeks with the pain in the right shoulder and was treated with inflammation. In Jan 1999 his cough is getting worse and this appetite is decreased and fatigure and getting weak. On CT there is mass on the right upper lung showing the central lung. He had endoscope and biopsy which showed that lung adenocarcinoma in the xxxxxx. He and his family member don't want to have operation. In Feb 1999 after chemotherapy for one course, his reaction to the chemotherapy was strong and stopped to use it. This patient had metastasis in the left lung which showed there are two lesions and he coughed with mucous and blood sputdu and difficult walking. On April 23 2000 he started to take the XZ-C1+XZ-C4+XZ-C7, LMS+MDZ for three months and his general condition is good and he is lively and his appetite is great. In December 2000 his medical condition is stable, and he is lively. His appetite is good and his breath is smooth and his face is red. He walked as the normal person and sometimes he coughs. He persistently takes this medication for more than four years and when he comes back to follow up during the five years, his general condition is great and he walked as the normal healthy person.

Comments: this patient has the central lung cancer in the right upper lung. In April 2000 he started to use XZ-C1+XZ-C4+XZ-C7. XZ-C1 is used to kill the cancer cells only without kill the normal cells; XC-C4 protect the thymus and increase the thymus weight and to protect the bone marrow, XZ-C7 inhibit the lung cancer cells and protect the lung and solve the suptid. After short-term chemotherapy he started to take the XZ-C to strengthen his long-term therapy. XZ-C improve the whole body immune system and he is lively and his appetite is good and his spleen is great and help the patients against the diseases and help the patient's organ functions and the nutrition condition and metabliztion recover so that the patients' healthy condition is recovery.

This patient didn't have the operation. In Feb 1999 he had chemeotherapy, however there is left lung metastasis after chemotherapy. Afterh that,he only took the XZ-C to control the metastasis. He persistently took the medicine for more than four years and his medical condition is great without any complaints. He followed up with us for more than seven years. In May 2005 when he came back to follow up, his general medical condition is great and his appepital is good without other symptoms. His walking and activities and he talks cheerfully and humorously.

Case 2 Mrs. Huang, femal,66 year-old, Wuhan han yan, Medical record number:10102008

Diagnosis: the squamous carcinoma of the low esophagus

Disease courses and treatment: in December 2000 the patients started to vomit and to have progressively swallow difficultly and only swallow the half of xxxx food. EGD showed that there was narrow in the low esophagus, congestion, ulcer and xxx. Pathology showed squamous carcinoma in the lower esophagus. According to his medical condition he should be treated for a surgery, however because he could afford to the medical cost, he started to take XZ-C. After one month, he is energetic and his appetite is getting better and can eat the soft food, noodle and rice soup. After she continued to take these medicine for six months, he is vagour and his appetite is good and can eat the soft food and noodle and rice soup. Until June 2003 she took the medicine more than two and half years and his health condition is good and can eat the regular rice and felt fine as the normal healthy persons. However she stopped to taking the medicine for more than four and half months. Until Octocber 16 2003 he suddenly had the difficulties to swallow the food and vomit the brown food. She could not eat for more than three days. After adding her some fluids and continued to take XZ-C until Octocber 31 2003 she can eat the food again. After that, she never stopped taking the medicine again. Now she is 70 year-old and healthy the same as the normal persons. She is energetic and her appetite is good and can eat regular food. She lived in the seventh floor and everyday she will come down the first floor and sometimes she help others to fill the bicycle wheels.

Comments: This patient had the low grade squamous carcinoma in the low esophagaus which was diagnosed by EGC and pathology. At that time he could only eat the liquid food and half ofXXXX food. She makes her living by filling the bicycle wheels and didn't have money for her surgery so that she started to take XZ-C medicine. After taking the medicine half of year her symptoms turned good. Aftertaking the medicine two andhalf years she recovered as the normal person and didn't have any complain. Because of her incoming condition, she didn't get any other tests and treatment. When she came back to followup, she had taken the medicine more than five years and her condition is good.

To take XZ-C for longterm can improve the patients immune function and the pateitns energy level will increase and the appetites will increase and the sleep will be good. XZ-C4 can protect the bone marrow and thymus to improve the nutrition and the metabolism will turn good and will get rid of the free bases to control and to repair the diseases.

Case 3 Mrs Hang, female, 65year-old, Huangpi in Hubei, Medical record number:10402074

Diagnosis: the middle esophogus carcinoma

Disease courses and treatment condition: In April 2001 the patient had difficulty swallowing and chest and back pain and gradually increased. Until June only can eat the liquid food and vomit the mucous staffs. On June 6 2001 the barium swallow tests in the xxx showed under the aorta branch xxxx 2cm there is a 10cm lenghth narrow and 6cm xxxxxlump in the left wall and the muscous stop. Because of the cost, she didn't have the operation, radioactive and chemotherapy. On June 25 she started to take XZ-C. After three months, her general condition is better and her appetite is getting better and the difficultying swallowing is getting better and can eat the rice soup, noodle. She continued taking the medicine until March 2002 then can take the rice and regular food. In July 2003 she just took XZ-C4+XZ-C2. In April 2005 when she followed up with us, she is energetic and her appetites was great at that time she had been taking XZ-C for more than five year. He condition is stable and can eat the regular food and can do light house work.

Comments: This patient had esophageal cancer which she only took XZ-C to control her condition without the operation, radiactiv therapy and chemotherapy. For more than four years, there was no metastasis and her condition had been controlled and can eat the regular food and rice. She is as healthy as other old persons and can do some choresevery day.

She kept taking her medicine regularly.

Case 4 Ms. Liu, female, 65 year-old, Jianxian in Hubei, officer. Medical record number: 110201

Diagnosis: primary huge liver carcinoma

Disease course and treatment: Because of discomfort in upper abdomen, the patient had CT in XieHe hospital which found that a 6.7 cm x 7.1 cm x 9 cm nodule in right liver, then diagnosed as primary liver carcinoma. She refused to take operation and chemotherapy. In July 11, 1995 she started to take the XZ-C1+XZ-C5. After 2 months, her emotion and appetite get better and her weight increased. In September 20, 1995 on follow-up ultrasound, the nodule was reduced. In November 1995 she had a chemoembolization and didn't have any other therapy. She continues to take the XZ-C for more than 6 years and continues to follow-up more than 10 years. This patient's condition is good. In May 2005 this patient is as healthy as a normal person.

Comments: On July 4, 1995 this patient was diagnosed with primary liver carcinoma by CT and then took XZ-C after 1 week. After 2 month, the CT scan showed that the nodule become smaller. On November 21 the chemotherapy procedure was conducted, and then she continued to take XZ-C regularly and persistently for 10 years. Now this patient is as healthy as a normal individual.

Implication: The chemotherapy+XZ-C have good results on liver carcinoma treatment. The chemotherapy can stop the blood supply to the cancer nodule and chemotherapy can kill some of the cancer cells. There are living cancer cells inside and under the tumor nodule membrane after chemotherapy; the tumor cells didn't die completely and then grew fast after circulation built up. XZ-C can protect thymus and improve the immune ability, protect the bone morrow function and improve the body immune function. In addition, 85% hepatic cancer occurred in the cirrhosis patients so chemotherapy will damage the liver function. XZ-C will protect the liver. The combination of chemotherapy+XZ-C will inhibit the tumor and protect the host to improve the long-term treatment. This is called "take out the bad and keep the good" in Chinese.

Case 5. Mr. Huang, male, 53 year-old, Wuhan. Medical record number: number: 11202225
Diagnosis: primary huge liver cancer, liver cirrhosis after hepatitis, the later stage of Japanese blood fluke, Portal hypertension.

Disease course and treatment: Patient's appetite decreased and he felt uncomfortable in his abdomen. In September 2000 CT showed a 13.6cm x 11.8cm lesion in the right liver lobe. In September 7, 2000 MRI showed a huge 13.1cm x 11.4cm x 12.5cm lesion in right lobe, diagnosed as huge liver cancer in right lobe. The patient had hepatic arterial chemoembolization (HACE) and embolization (HAE) and the chemoembolization medicine were xxxx 25mg+xxx1000g: xxxx10ml+xxxx10mg. Currently his general condition is good. The change of his liver lesions are the following which are stable and getting small: CT showed a 11.1cm x 11.8cm lesion in the right liver lobe on October 12, 2000, a 10.8cm x 9.8cm lesion in the right liver lobe on December 14, 2000, a 10.5cm x 9.5cm lesion on Feb 2001 and a 9.8cm x 8.9cm lesion on September 3, 2001 in the right liver lobe. This patient started to take XZ-C1+XZ-C4+XZ-C5 on January 9, 2002 and his general condition is good, just as his emotion, appetite and sleep are very good. He comes back for check-up every month and takes his medicine regularly. On October 21, 2002 during his follow-up, his general condition is good, emotion is stable, and appetite is good and bowel movement is good and his routine is regular and he exercises regularly. He reports not having had a cold during the last four years. He lived as a normal healthy person.

Comments: This case is primary huge liver carcinoma which had five times embolization and the lesion was getting smaller and had very good response. Last embolization is on November 12, 2001 and the lesion is 9.8cm x 8.9cm. He started to take XZ-C1+XZ-C4+XZ-C5 on Jan 9, 2002. The XZ-C1 can kill the cancer cells and not kill the normal cells; XZ-C4 protects thymus and inhibits thymus shrinkage; XZ-C5 protects liver function. This patient continues to take this medicine for more than 3 years, however when he came back for follow-up in the fourth year, his health condition is general, disease is stable and there is no metastasis and no further development. His emotion is stable, his appetite is good, and he walks as a normal healthy person. The experience from this case is for primary huge liver cancer, first embolization treatment are given to make this lesion smaller and stable, later use XZ-C to support the long-term therapy and to protect the liver function and to improve the immune system and to control the metastasis.

Case 6. Mr. Pu, male, 51 year-old, Yin Zheng, officer. Medical record number: number: 500989
Diagnosis: primary liver cancer

Disease course and treatment: There is a 4.6cm x 3.6cm nodule in left liver and a 1.6cm x 1.6cm nodule in right liver after the patient had CT on October 30, 1997. Diagnosis was liver carcinoma. There is a 5.9cm x 4.0cm x 5.4cm nodule in the left liver lobe and a 2.1cm x 1.8cm lesion in the right liver lobe when the patient had Ultrasound in the XieHe hospital. Liver angiography showed that the patient had liver cancer. HBsAg(+), AFP(-). Because this patient's liver function was poor, he couldn't stand the operation and put on the tube for chemotherapy. This patient is alcohol drinker for 40 years (250ml/per meal average). In 1996 he had Hepatitis B. In 1966 he had blood fluke. On November 25 the patient starts to take XZ-C1+XZ-C4+XZ-C5. In 1998 and 1999 the patient continued to take the medicine. The patient's condition is good, and his face is red and smiles. On November 2, 1999 he came to follow-up and the ultrasound showed the lesion was reduced. He can do light work and feels very well. For more than 2 years, he continues to take XZ-C1+XZ-C4+XZ-C5. After these medicines the patient's energy level is improving and appetite is improving. In June 2002 he went to Beijing for treatment (before he went to Beijing, he was good and walking as the normal person). During the operation there is a 5cm x 6cm nodule in the liver which is the same as 5 years ago and there are cancer cells in the common duct and now metastasis, and no fluid in the abdominal cavity. There is no metastasis in the liver, however because the nodule is close to the hepatic artery entrance, it is very difficult to remove the cancer nodule and then place the drainage tube. After surgery, this patient didn't have urine and had acute renal failure. He passed away on day 6.

Comments: On October 30, 1997 CT showed a 4.6cm x 3.6cm nodule in left liver and in November 1997 there is a 1.6cm x 1.6cm nodule in right liver. Because the liver function was poor, the patient didn't have operation and tube placement and other treatment. On November 25 he started to take XZ-C1+XZ-C4+XZ-C5 and continued for 5 years. His health condition was fine.

Implication: XZ-C can improve the host immune system ability (including the cell and antibody immune function) to protect the central and peripheral immune organs, to protect the liver and kidney, and to produce anticancer factors an dprevent cancer cells metastasis and spread. XZ-C is a medication with no side effects which helps the patient in "fight with bad and help the right". In addition the patient's disease condition was under very good control without metastasis so that therapeutic effect was very good. This patient took XZ-C for 5 years, during which time his condition was stable and the liver cancer lesion was not increasing and there were no metastasis. His general condition was good and not uncomfortable and the patient walked as a normal person. He went to Beijing and was diagnosed as liver cells carcinoma which was in the entrance of the liver and couldn't be removed because of the cancer cells in the common duct. The patient underwent surgery for the placement of the T-tube for chemotherapy. After the operation, this patient didn't have urine and died of acute renal failure. If he had not had the operation which destroyed the liver and kidney function, he might have survived to the present day.

二. The Typical Case with XZ-C immune regulation and control anti-cancer medication for the patient who the surgical exploration cannot remove tumor, nor do radiotherapy and chemotherapy

Case 1 Mr.Cheng, male, 64 year-old Hubei Xin Zhou, officer, Medical record number: 7301454

Diagnosis: the tumor of the mesentaic membranexxxx.

Disease courses and treatment condition:On January 6 1999 the patient suddenly had the uncomfortable in chest and pain and vomit. The emergency diagnosis was "actual GI infection", the surgeons thought of that he had the pancreatitis. On March 3 EGD showed the obstractle of the duodenum. On March 6 1999 during the survey of the abdomen, the tumor which was behind the abdominal membrance including big vessals which during the operation a 6cmx9cm lump in the roots of the small intestine membreance xxxx of hard, stable, fixed and unsmooth on the surface, connected to aorta and the xxxx arterial and pressed the duodenum which it was difficult to remove so that the connection of the duodenus and colon was done because the tumor can not be removed and the patients was told to be treated by the combination of the western and Chinese therapy. On April 1999 she started to take XZ-C1Z+C4. From May 15 1999 to February 2002 she continued to take the medicine and refill her medicine. She is stable and her medical condition is good.

Comments: On March 6 1999 the tumor from the abdomen membrane was foundby the survey of the operation. Because it is connected to the small intestine membrance including the big artery, this tumor can not be removed. But the surface of the tumor was firm and stable, which implied malignant. After taking Z-C years, the patients is stable and no development and no metastasis and healthy.

Case 2. Mr. Fong, male, 50 year-old, Hubei Lou Tang, peasant. Medical record number: 330651

Diagnosis: Pancreas cancer

Disease course and treatment: Because of discomfort in upper abdomen for more than three months, he had jaundice and had opening abdomen surgery showing: No stones in the bile system and enlargement of the pancreas. The tumor couldn't be removed and Pathology showed pancreatic cancer. CT showed enlargement of pancreas head and dilation of the bile duct in liver. After the operation the jaundice extended persistently. On December 11, 1996 he started to take the XZ-C and after one month his medical condition got better and his appetite increased, however he still had little jaundice and weakness and sweating. After taking XZ-C and soup two months the jaundice and pain reduced and got better. After four months, the jaundice was gone completely and his appetite and energy level were good. His pain in abdomen was mild. In July 1998 he returned to work and did mild labor work and his face looks red. He continues to take his medicine for many years. On April 6, 2004 his family introduced a new patient to us and told us that this patient is fine and his activities are as a normal person's and he does his chores very well.

Comments: This patient has pancreas head cancer and jaundice. On November 28 1996 during the operation, this tumor cannot be removed and the Pathology is pancreas cancer with the dilation of the bile duct system in the livers. On December 11, 1996 this patient took ZX-C and soup. After seven months his jaundice is reduced and he continues to take medicine to improve his immune system. Until July 1998 his condition is completely normal. He continues to take his medicine for more than four years and later changed to taking the medicine periodically to support his healthy condition. This patient has followed up for more than nine years and his condition is very good

Case 3. Mr. Lee, male, 53 year-old, Wuhan, farmer. Medical record number: 9901979
Diagnosis: primary huge liver carcinoma, late stage Japanese blood fluke hepatic cirrhosis.

Disease course and treatment: On January 22, 2001 the patient felt pain in the right back. In Feb 26, 2001 ultrasound showed a nodule in the liver. On January 31, 2001 CT showed a

14cm x 1cm lesion in the right liver lobe diagnosed as primary huge liver cancer in the right liver. On March 1, 2001 the open abdomen surgery was done in Tongjin Hospital and the pump implantation in the portal vein because the lesion was huge and couldn't be removed. After the surgery the patient received chemotherapy once. This patient had 30 years Japanese blood fluke. On March 9, 2001 this patient started to take XZ-C medicine. He used XZ-C1+XZ-C4+XZ-C5, LMS, MDZ, and XZ-C3 placed on a fist-size lump in the right rib edge area. After one month of taking this medicine, the patient's condition is getting better and his emotion is stable and happy. His appetite is increasing. The lump in the right rib edge area is getting smaller and softer than before. After he continued to take this medicine for three months, his general condition is good and his appetite and sleep are good. His energy level is recovering and he is walking as a normal person. On October 22, 2001 Ultrasound showed a 6cm x 7.8cm lesion in the right lobe liver and he continues taking XZ-C1+XZ-C4+XZ-C5 and using XZ-C3 on the lump. On November 19, 2003 during his follow-up, ultrasound showed this lesion size the same as before, kidney function is normal and CXR didn't show abnormality, there is no positive lymph node and the lump on the right rib edge is soft and getting smaller and the boundry is clear and not painful. This patient continued to use XZ-C1+XZ-C4+XZ-C5.

Comments: This case is diagnosed as primary huge liver cancer and the lesion can not be removed so that the portal vein pump was placed for chemotherapy once. In March 2001, he started to use the XZ-C1+XZ-C4+XZ-C5 and topical XZ-C3 for 4 years. His general condition is stable and didn't develop further and didn't metastasize.

Case 4. Mr. Kei, male, 54 year-old, Yanxi in Hubei, officer. Medical record number: number: 6301244.

Diagnosis: primary liver carcinoma

Disease course and treatment: The patient had pain on the upper right abdomen for half of a month and his appetites decreased. CT in Yanxia showed nodules in the right front and back lobe and left lobe. The patient was diagnosed with primary liver carcinoma. On August 20, 1998 the patient had opening surgery which revealed that the main tumors were in the entrance of the common duct and there were metastasis in both of left and right liver, which could not be removed. Therefor a tube for the chemotherapy was placed through the hepatic artery. After the operation, the chemotherapy was used once. In October 1998 the second chemotherapy was used. Because the tube was blocked, the patient stopped using the tube. On September 8, 1998 he started taking XZ-C1+XZ-C4+XZ-C5. After taking this medicine one month, the patient's emotion and appetite were good and his body weight increased and his face was glowing with health. On his physical exam the abdomen was soft and flat and the spleen and liver could not be felt; his general condition was good. He could support himself very well and picked up his medication by himself. On June 4, 2002 when he came back for his follow-up, his healthy condition was good; his face was glowing with health, his walking, acting and smiling were like a normal, healthy person. On the physical exam there was no abnormality found.

Comments: On August 20, 1998 liver carcinoma was found in the right and left liver and could not be removed, and a chemotherapy tube was placed, through which the chemotherapy was twice given after CT scan showed many lesions in the left lobe, right front and right back lobe.

On September 8 the patient started to take XZ-C1+XZ-C4+XZ-C5. Until 2002 this patient's condition was good and didn't have metastasis.

Implication: When liver cancer could not be removed, the liver artery tube could be placed, then XZ-C1+XZ-C4+XZ-C5 was used to protect Thymus, bone morrow, liver to improve the host immune system function and induce the host to produce more anticancer factors to control the tumors and to control the development of the cancers

三. **The Typical cases for recurrence after radical surgery, with Z-C immunomodulatory anticancer medicine treatment**

Case 1 Mr. Mao, male, 48 year-old, Taimen, officer. Medical record number: 100014 Diagnosis: Primary liver carcinoma

Disease course and treatment: On August 1, 1994 because the patient felt fatigued, he had ultrasound in the local hospital and found a 4.1cm x 4.5cm nodule in the left lobe of the liver. On August 26, 1994 the left lobe of the liver was removed in the Xian Ha hospital. Pathological slides showed: liver cell carcinoma without any treatment. After operation, the patient was treated with anticancer immunological traditional medicine **XZ-C1+XZ-C4+XZ-C5** in our outpatient center. After taking these medicines, the patient's appetite increased, energy level increased and he was happy. He takes medicines regularly and comes to our office every month for follow up and refilling of the medicines. He feels very well and goes back to his work. On December 14, 1996 there was another 1.3cm x 1.8cm nodule which was found by B ultrasound in the edge of the left liver. On December 30, 1996 he had that nodule removed. After the operation, he continued to take the medicine. After that, the patient took his medicine persistently and regularly. In May 2010 when he came to follow-up, his general condition was good and his face was glowing with health, his body was as strong as a healthy person's and the patient returned to work for more than 11 years. His appetite is great and his emotion is very good. He eats 600g food per day and his ultrasound is normal.

Comments. On August 26, 1994 this patient had a 4.1cm x 4.5cm nodule removal of left liver. After the operation, the patient received XZ-C for treatment. On December 30, 1996 another 1.3cm x 1.8cm nodule was found and removed. After that, this patient continued to take XZ-C. When he came back for 16-year follow-up, his health condition is good and he can do labor work for many years. This patient is still alive and very well at the time of writing this book.

Case 2 Mr. Chan, male, 65 year-old, Wuhan, retired officer. Medical record number: 280555

Diagnosis: Adenocarcinoma in the pyloric area of the stomach and recurrence after surgery in the remaining stomach

Disease course and treatment: This patient had pain in the upper abdomen for more than one year and in June 1993 he was diagnosed as stomach cancer and had removal of the great curvature in the stomach. After the operation, he had FM chemotherapy once which caused anemia and weakness and wbc is 1900. 8 months after operation, the patient had abdomen pain with vomiting and had left upper abdominal pain for half year. On March 25, 1994 the Barium showed: there was no filled on the upper area of the stomach and part damage of the membranes and the narrow change in the cutting parts. A barium swallow showed recurrence of the stomach cancer. On May 3, 1996 ultrasound showed that there is no lesion inside the liver. Because this patient couldn't eat rice and just eats noodles and liquid food so that he had fatigue and no energy, he didn't want to have operation. In June 1996 he started to take XZ-C. After that he is fine and his appetite is increased and he takes this medicine regularly for more than four years. On May 6, 2000 when he came back to follow-up, his general condition is great and his face looks red and healthy. Walking and activities are normal as the others and he eats rice soup and banana often as his meal.

Comments: In June 1993 the patient had stomach removal. In March 1994 the cancer recurred and the junction part turned narrow. After taking XZ-C+XZ-C4 only, for more than six years his health condition is great.

Implication: For the recurrence of the stomach cancers, the junction of the surgery was not closed completely and the patient could still eat food. After taking the medicines to improve thymus function to control the tumor growth and prevent the tumor growth and metastasis XXXX. The patient's medical condition is stable and he is still alive.

Case 3: Mr. Cheng, male, 62year-old, Wuhan, engineer, Medical record number:s: 210412

Diagnosis: Renal pelvis carcinoma in the right kidney and the recurrence after the bladder carcinoma operation.

Diseases courses and treatment: the patient had cytoscopy which showed the bladder carcinoma in November 4 1995 afterthe bloody urine for two years. On November 21 1995 CT showed that rght renal pelvis tumor. On December 6 1995 the right kidney and urother were removed and his bladder was removed by the xxx and after the operation the local xxxx chemotherapy was used for seven times. On March 8 1996 the cystoscopy showed there was the hard lump in the left wall of the bladder in order to prevent the reccurrence of the tumor, he started to take XZ-C1+XZ-C4+XZ-C6. After taking this medicine he is well and his appetite is getting better. On June 24 1996 the cytoscopy showed that the bladder walls are smooth and the surface is smooth and the new things were gone. He continued to take XZ-C medicine to prevent the recerence and metastasis. Until June 11 1997 the cystoscopy showed the bladder is normal. On December 28 1998 the cystoscopy is normal. On June 26 1999 when he came back to follow up, his condition is stable and he continues to take the XZ-C1+XZ-C4+XZ-C6 for more than ten years to prevent the recurrence and metastasis. On May 6 2005 when he follow-up, he is stable and his condition is good and is the same as the normal individuals.

Comments: this case is the recurrence of the bladder cancinoma after the operation. After taking this medicine more than ten years to prevent the recurrence and metastasis, his medical condition is good and after many cystoscopy, the bladder is normal.

Suggestion: XZ-C can improve the patients immune function and prevent the tumor recurrence and metastasis and control the primary lesions. He is healthy and is in the good condition.

Case 4. Mr. Lin, male, 68year-old, Wuhan, Professor, Medical record number:: 7701534

Diagnosis: the recurrence of the bladder cancer operation.

Disease courses and treatment conditions: After the removal of the bladder cancer was done in April 1994 in the hospital, Pathology showed: transitional cell carcinoma. After the operation the bladder was poured with chemotherapy. Because of the decrease of the white blood cells the chemotherapy stopped. In 1996 he came back to check up and found the cancer recurrence so that the second operation was done by the removal of eight tumors. After the surgery the patient's bladder was poured with XXX+XXXX twice every month for three months. After three months, repeat these medicine for another three months. Twice per month until 1997. In May 1998 the cystoscopy in the XXX hospital showed the xxx in the bladder. In December the ultrasound showed the bladder infection. In April 1999 because of the bloody urine, the cystoscopy showed that there were a four cm2 of the tumor and CT biopsy showed that bladder cancer. In May 1999 the arterial chemotherapy was poured. In June the second time of the poured the XXXX+XXXX+XXX was done. After that the white blood cells decreased into 2x109/l. In September the third time of the poured medicine with xxx+xxxx+xxx, the white blood cells decreased into 1.2x109/L, then inject the XXX to increase the white blood cells. His medical history: stroke in 1992, Hypertension(160/90mmHg), Diabete. In 1984 he had hepatitis and in 1998 had cirrhosis. Family history : two brothers had hepatitis B and then liver cancer, another brother had rectal cancer.

In July 1999 because of the white blood cells decrease after the chemotherapy, he started to take xxxx to protect the bone marrow and take XZ-C1+XZ-C4+XZ-C6. After taking them more than six months, the whole blood count come back again. His energy level is increased and his appetite is getting better and continue taking the medicine. In July 2000 the cystoscopy showed that the bladder was filled well and a 1.3cmx0.6cm xxxxx in the xxxx ranges, considering as the recurrence of the tumors and continued to take the medicine until June 2001, because of the prostate enlargement which caused the frequency and urgency of the urine CT showed that this lesion was getting bigger than before(in February in 1999), then had arterialy poured once. He continued to take XZ-C1+XZ-C4+XZ-C6 untill July 2002 CT showed that the lesion in CT shrinkled. After taking the medicine, his general medical condition is better and his appetites is good without the bloody urine. He kept coming back to followup and take his medicine for more than six years. His lesion in his bladder is stable without metastasis and enlargement.

Comments: This case is transitional cell carcinoma. After the removal of the cancer, the long- time chemotherapy didn't stop the recurrence. Because of many years of the poured bladder and many times of the cystoscopy with the enlargement of the prostate and the narrowness of the urother, the cystescopy is difficult to be done. After taking XZ-C such as XZ-C1+XZ-C4+XZ-C6, the neoplasm in the bladder didn't develop and didn't metastes. Since he had this disease, it has been 11 years. His general medical condition is well and his appetite is getting better. When he walked more, sometimes the bloody urine occurred.

Case 5 Mrs. Pu, female, 67year-old,Shiyiazhoung, worker, Medical record number::7601511.

Diagnosis: The recurrence after the surgery of the abdominal cavity serous tumors

Disease courses and treatment conditions:because of the belly was getting bigger and ascites, in May 1999 he was hosptilized in Tongjing and ascite(++) and his belly was like to frog and the tumor can be touched. On April 9 the surgery found that there were very many different sizes of the tumor, which were gel-like lump full of the abdominal cavity. One by one were removed, the total weight are 2.5g. During the operations, the chemotherapy tube was put with XXX 500mg. After the operation of four days xxx500MG once/per day and continued to use five days and xxx 100mg once/per day and continuing three days. On June 16 1999 he started to take XZ-C1+XZ-C4 andd after two months she is vigour and her appetite is good and her weight increases. PE: there were no lymph nodes in the superclavial, the abdomen is soft and flat, the ascite(-) and continue to take the XZ-C and refilled her medicine every month until November 26 2000, PE: there was a lump of the fit=size, hard, many nodual on the surface and deep and the clear edges which showed the tumor recurrence. The patient refused to the operation again and to chemotherapy, however he continued to take the XZ-C medicine: XZ-C1+XZ-C4+LMS+MDZ and the anticancer gel on the skin patched. Until Febrauay 24 2002 PE: there was on abnormal and her abdomen was soft and there was a lump which was hard, deep and clear edge and the size is smaller than before and her medical condition is stable. Until December 15 2004 her medical condition is good and her appetite is good and her abdomen is little enlarge and her ascite(++) and there is a fit-size lump with unsmooth surface and many nodule and deep and fix without the metastasis further. After her operation until now she has been following up with us more than six years and her medical condition is stable and the tumor is not metasatasis further.

Comments: This case is the serous tumor in the abdominal cavity. After the removal, the tumor recurrence. After the chemotherapy one week, the reaction is great so that in June 1999 she started to take XZ-C1+XZ-C3+XZ-C4 and she continued to take this medicine for more than six years and her medical condition is stable without the far metastasis and the tumors didn't grow big. She lives well with the tumors.

四. The typical cases of extensive bone metastasis, with Z-C immunomodulatory anticancer medicine treatment

Case 1 Mrs Pan, female,68year-old, Shengyang

Diagnosis: multiple bone metastasis after the removal of the breast cancer.

Disease courses and treatment: in 1984 the patient had the removal of the right breast cancer I stage, the pathology showed that simple breast cancer without lymph node metastasis. After the xxx +xxxx chemotherapy for two years, she started to use some immune enhancing drug. In January 2001 she felt the right shoulder pain and ECT showed that multiple bone metastasis and the supericlavical lymph nodes enlargement. Since March 27 she had 25 times radicacto therapy on the sites of the right superoclaviceal lymph nodes and the whole blood counts decreases and the white cell counts decrease into 2.9x109/L. After the radiactherapy, her condition stable.

On June 15 2001 he started to take XZ-C such XZ-C1+XZ-C2+XZ-C4+LMS+MDZ+VS for two months and her symptom significantly increased. After six months ECT was normal and she is stable. On September 2 2002 on the phone she told us that she is stable and takes her medicine regularly for more than four years. In April 2005 She called us that she is energetic and her appetites is great and walking as the normal healthy persons. On her physical examination, Ultrasound of her liver and gallbladder,Chest X-ray, ECT etc she is normal.

Comments:this patient had right breast cancer after the operation for more than 17 years with bone metastasis and right shoulder pain. After the radiactiv therapy her medical condition is getting better. After taking XZ-C for a long period to protect thymus and bone marrow function, her metastasis was controlled well.

Case 2 Mr. Zhong, male, 66 year-old, Wuxiu, officer, Medical record number:: 11602315

Diagnosis: right kidney clear cell tumors with the bone marrow metastasis and superclavaical lymph node metastasis.

Disease courses and treatment condition: Because of the pain in the right should, the diagnosis was "the inflamtion of the sourround shoulder", which there was a lump as big as XXX behind the right clavical and stern bone, the biopsy showed adenocarcinoma. After CT of abdomen and chest Ultrasound, there was no lesion found. On March 2002 he started to take the XZ-C such as taking XZ-C1+XZ-C4 and plastic XZ-C3. After the plastic gels, the lump was getting soft and shrinkle into small. On March 24 2002 Ultrasound showed a lump of 3.1cmx4.3cm in the right kidney. CT showed : L2,L4 had bone damage and still took the XZ-C and GEM+XXX chemotherapy once. On May 16 2002 the right renal was removed which there was a lump of the size of table tennis. Pathology showed clear cells. Because he was on the immune function medicine, his medical condition was stable and his appetite is good. Although he had the metastasis of his whole body, he still walked as the normal persons. In 2002,2003 and 2004 he came back every month to refill his medicine and his medical condition is stable. Until July 2004 he suddenly lost the ability of speech and headache. CT showed that the bleeding of the brain. After three weeks of the hospitalization,his medical condition was stable and CT showed that the brain bleeding was absorbed and he continues to take XZ-C1+XZ-C2+XZ-C6+LMS+XXX+XXX+xxxx etc. His medical condition is good and he is vigour and his appetite is good.

Comments: this case is the right metastasis lump of the clavic bone with L2 and L4 bone metastasis, the biopsy showed the metastasis adenocarcinoma. After the whole examination the right kidney tumor was found. On May 16 2002 he was diagnosed as right kidney clear cell cancer and the kidney was removed. On March 16 2002 he started to use the XZ-C by taking and plastic. After three years his medical condition is stable and his appetite is good and he is vigour.

五. The cases of simply using Z-C anti-cancer traditional Chinese medicine after radical surgery without chemotherapy and radiotherapy

Case 1 Ms Liu, female, 49 year-old, Changsha in Hunan, teacher, Medical record number::260003372

Diangosis: breast infiltrating ductal cancer.

Disease courses and treatment condition: in February 2005 a left breast lump was found which is 2cmx1.5cm, biopsy showed that high degree mutation. On March 8 2005 she had CAF.

On May 30 2005 the breast cancer was removed partially, pathology showed the breast cancer so that the breast cancer radiact removal was performed Pathologyshowed that left breast cancer infiltrated ductal cancer. LN0/20 with the C-erB2(++), P53(+), PR(-),ER(-),nm23(+). After the surgery the chemotherapy was used for six cycles. On Octocber 22 2005 she started to take XZ-C to strengthen the curative effects and to prevent the recurrence and metastasis.

Comments:in this case before the operation the lymph nodes under armpit were palpatited. Chemotherapy for six cycle was used before the operation and after the operations to strengthen the long time curative effect. She persistently takes these medicine more than six years and her healthy condition is stable.

Case 2 Mr. Yan, female, 71 year-old, Wuhan, teacher, Medical record number:s:100188
Diagnosis: ascending colon carcinoma

Disease courses and treatment: Because of abdomen pain and bloody stool, the patient was diagnosed as colon cancer by colonoscopy with biopsy. On December 19 1994 he had half of the right colon removal. Pathology showed the medium grade of colon adenocarcinoma involved in serosa. After the operation, he didn't accept other therapy. On July 4 1995 he started to take XZ-C1+XZ-C4 as assistant therapy to prevent the recurrence and metastasis. He only takes XZ-C more than ten years and his healthy condition is very good. In April 2005 when he was 81 years old and came back to follow up with us, he was healthy and played the card every day in the afternoon.

Comments: this case is that after the removal of the ascending colon, the patient just takes XZ-C medicine as the assistant therapy to protect recurrence more than 10 years and his condition is stable.

Case3 Mr. Zhou, male, 49year-old, Wuhan, officer, Medical record number:s: 410804
Diagnosis: lung cancer in the right low labor

Disease courses and treatment: In 1996 the patient started to have cough and chest tightness and low fever and difficult breath and was treated as the Cold. In April 1997 he suddenly started to cough blood and X-ray and CT showed the right lung cancer in low lobe. And at the same month he had right low lobe lung removal and Pathology showed that lung low grade adenocarcinoma. After the operation, his condition is stable and didn't have chemotherapy and radioactive therapy. On May 15 1997 he started to take XZ-C:1,4,7,vitamin C,B6 E,A. After he took these medicine his energy level is increase and appetite was great and his face is red and there were no recuurence and metastasis and no complaints. In June 2004, the patient came back to follow up with us

he continues to take these medicine more than three years. Everything is stable. So far his condition is stable as the normal healthy person after he took his medication more than eight years.

Comments: this patient has right low lobe low grade adenocarcinoma. After the operation, he didn't have radioactive and chemotherapy treatment and he only takes the XZ-C medication XZ-C1+C4+C7. After taking these medicine more than eight years, his energy level is high and appetite is good and his healthy condition is great.

Case 4 Mr. Zheng, male, 52 year-old, Wuhan, driver, Medical record number::11302254

Diagnosis: right lung low grade adenocarcinoma with lymph node metastasis

Disease courses and treatment: because of bloody cough he had the CTscan which showed that right low lung tumor and the bronchoscopy didn't show abnormal. On December 12 2001 he had the removal of the right middle and lower lobe and one lymph node between lobe and two lymph node in the entrance were found. Pathology showed that low grade adenocarcinoma with lymph node mestastasis. After the operation he has once chemotherapy. In 2002 he started to take XZ-C to prevent the tumor recurrence and metastasis. He continues to take the XZ-C1+C4+C7+LMS+MDZ for more than three year and his condition is stable and he is energetic and his appetite is great.

Comments: this patient has the right low lobe adenocarcinoma with lymph node metastasis. After the chemotherapy once, then using the XZ-C1+C4+C7 as the supplement treatment. XZ-C1 kills the cancer cells without killing the normal cells. XZ-C4 protects the thymus and bone marrow; XZ-C7 to protect the lung function. He continues to take his medication for more than three years and there was not metatastasis. When he came back to follow up for his fourth year treatment, his condition is stable and his appetite is great and walked as the normal healthy person.

Case 5 Mr. Yin, female, 60 yr, Huangpu, Medical record number::8301655

Diagnosis: sigmoid colon cancer and the removal of half of the left colon.

Disease courses and treatment: In August 1998 the patient had bloody stool and was treated as hemorrhoid. In Octocber 1999 when he had the colonoscopy in Xiehu hospital which there is narrow in the 32cm from the anus. On December 3 1999 he had the removal of half of the left-colon. Pathology showed:sigmoid xxxx adenocarcinoma involved in the whole layers of the colon and the metastasis of the nearby lymph nodules(6/8). On Jan 12 2000 he started to take XZ-C: XZ-C1+XZ-C4+LMS+MDA+VT to protect recurrence and metastasis. After he continues to take the XZ-C more than three years and eight months, his son came to refill the medicine on August 4 2003 and told us that his medical condition was good and did the chores every day and planted a lot of different kinds of flowers and vegatables watering them with ten buckles of water. The patient has been in the good condition and happy and has good energy. After his operation, he continues to take the XZ-C medicines only everyday without other chemotherapy. When he followed up with us, he already took the medicine more than five and half years.

Comments: the case is that sigmoid colon carcinoma with metastasis of the nearby lymph nodes. After the removal of the operation the patient didn't have chemotherapy because of the decrease of the white blood cells so that he took the XZ-C as the assistant therapy to protect the bone morrow and thymus to improve the body immune system to protect the reccurrence and the metastasis. After five and half years, his condition was good.

Case 6 Ms. Yun, female, 63year-old, Jiling, officer, Medical record number::8601705

Diagnosis: the rectal adenocarcinoma

Disease courses and treatment: in Octocbor 1999 the patient has the bloody stool and the the rectaoscopy showed there is a flower-like tumor in the 10cm distance from the ana and Pathology showed the rectal cancer. On November 22 1999 the rectal radioactive surgery was done in the affliatite hospital with Dixon ways. After the operation the patient's condition is stable. On December 2 the chemotherapy was done(urine xxxx 1.0g/day, for five days, xxx 100mg/day for three days). On December 9 the white blood cell counts decrease into 0.09x109/L, on December 10 the white blood cells decrease into 0.06x109/L, injection of the medicine of increasing the white blood cells for five days, the white blood cells into1.1x109/l and had the pneumonia and fever with 40C. On January 2 xxxx after treatment with xxxx+xxxx, the patient still has fever and had the throat infection with three bacteria and can not eat and drink anything. After using XXX for five days, the temperature dropped into 38C. Because this patient had hypertension, diabetes and lung diseases, her medical condition is weak and severe and had twice warrancy from the hospitals. After two months of the treatment, she is stable. On March 20 2000 she started to take XZ-C for half of the years and her medical condition is stable and can do a little chores and can support her daily life by her own. On September 2000 she recurred very well and can shop in the nearby market and do little chores. She has been taken the medicine for more than five years consistently. In May 2005 her daughter come to refill the medicine and told us that she is totally fine and still do some house chores as healthy as other normal healthy individuals.

Comments: this case is the radial rectal cancer removal and the chemotherapy. After these her immune function and bone morrow function were inhibited so that she had throat and both the lung infections, which later are two fungus infections. After the treatment her condition started to get better and started to take the XZ-C which XZ-C1 only inhibited the tumor cells without affecting the normal cells and improve the immune fucntions, XZ-C4 to protect thymus and bone marrow to improve the immune function. The chemotherapy can inhibit the bone marrow so as to lead the bone marrow inhibition to some degrees which can affect the patients for more than 2 to 3 years so that XZ-C which have protect thymus and bone marrow function need to be taken for several years to benefit the bone marrow and immune functions

Case 7 Ms Pen, female, 39 year-old, Shichuang Luchang, officer, Medical record number::7801545

Diagnosis: Thyroid cancer

Disease course and treatment: On April 27 1999 after the removal of the right neck lump, diagnosed as lymphocyte thyroid cancer. On May 6 1999 he had the radical total removal of the thyroid, then he had hourse voice and didn't have chemotherapy. On July 24 he started to take XZ-C:XZ-C1+XZ-C4, LMS,VS and follow-up with us every month and continue to use more than half years. Until Jan 2000 his voice gets better and after continue to take XZ-C another three months his voice come back to the normal. His general conditions get better and his emotion is stable and appetite is good and his energy level came back and he can go back his work. He persistently takes XZ-C1+XZ-C4 to improve his immune function and followed with us more six years and in May 2005 when he came back to us, his general condition is very good.

Comments: this patient has capillary thyroid cancer. After operation his voice was housral and didn't have radiology and chemoactive therapy. He only took the XZ-C to improve his immune function and to prevent recurrence and metastasis.

Case 8 Mrs. Pu, female, 67year-old,Shiyiazhoung, worker, Medical record number::7601511.

Diagnosis: The recurrence after the surgery of the abdominal cavity serous tumors

Disease courses and treatment conditions:because of the belly was getting bigger and ascites, in May 1999 he was hosptilizated in Tongjing and ascite(++) and his belly was like to frog and the tumor can be touched. On April 9 the surgery found that there were very many different sizes of the tumor, which were gel-like lump full of the abdominal cavity. One by one were removed, the total weight are 2.5g. During the operations, the chemotherapy tube was put with XXX 500mg. After the operation of four days xxx500MG once/per day and continued to use five days and xxx 100mg once/per day and continuing three days. On June 16 1999 he started to take XZ-C1+XZ-C4 andd after two months she is vigour and her appetite is good and her weight increases. PE: there were no lymph nodes in the superclavial, the abdomen is soft and flat, the ascite(-) and continue to take the XZ-C and refilled her medicine every month until November 26 2000, PE: there was a lump of the fit=size, hard, many nodual on the surface and deep and the clear edges which showed the tumor recurrence. The patient refused to the operation again and to chemotherapy, however he continued to take the XZ-C medicine: XZ-C1+XZ-C4+LMS+MDZ and the anticancer gel on the skin patched. Until Febrauay 24 2002 PE: there was on abnormal and her abdomen was soft and there was a lump which was hard, deep and clear edge and the size is smaller than before and her medical condition is stable. Until December 15 2004 her medical condition is good and her appetite is good and her abdomen is little enlarge and her ascite(++) and there is a fit-size lump with unsmooth surface and many nodule and deep and fix without the metastasis further. After her operation until now she has been following up with us more than six years and her medical condition is stable and the tumor is not metasatasis further.

Comments: This case is the serous tumor in the abdominal cavity. After the removal, the tumor recurrence. After the chemotherapy one week, the reaction is great so that in June 1999 she started to take XZ-C1+XZ-C3+XZ-C4 and she continued to take this medicine for more than six years and her medical condition is stable without the far metastasis and the tumors didn't grow big. She lives well with the tumors.

Case 9. Mr. Hc, male, 76year-old, Henan, officer, Medical record number:;9201839
Diagnosis: left renal clear cell cancer.

Disease courses and treatment condition:in 1996 there is a kidney cyst, in 2000 on PE there is a 7.5cmx6.5cm cysts in the left renal. CT and MRI showed that left kidney tumor. On August 31 2000 the removal of the left kidney was done in Tongjing hospital. Pathology showed that middle degree of kidney clear cells carcinoma. After the surgery he started to take the xxxx without chemotherapy and radiactvie therapy. On September 28 2000 she started to take XZ-C1+XZ-C4+XZ-C6 to protect thymus ad bone marrow. After taking the medicine one month, he is vigour and his appetite is still low and contine taking the medicine for three months, his general condition is good and his energy level is high and his sleeping is good. After taking the medicine for one year, Ultrasound of the abdomen, Chest X-ray, and others regular tests are normal and he continues to take XZ-C1+XZ-C4+XZ-C6 to prevent the metastasis and recurrence. After five years of taking these medicine, his healthy condition is stable. On April 10 2005 when he follow-up with us, he is healthy and his face is glowing of the health and his voice is xxxx, and he is energetic and had the hear decrease due to his age. His medical condition is100 by CCCCCC.

Comments: this case is left kidney clear cells. He was 76 year-old when he had his surgery. Because of his age, he didn't have the chemotherapy and radioactive therapy and only take the XZ-C immune therapy as the supplement therapy to protect his thymus and bone marrow to improve the immune functions and protect the recurrence and metastasits. He has been taking the medicine for more than five years and when he came back to followup he was 80 years old. His general medical condition is good and his appetite is good and his face is glowing of the health and his energy level is high and his voice is xxx as the normal healthy person.

Case 10 Mr. Zhen, female, 44 year-old, Wuhan, Medical record number:s: 700121

Diagnosis: Breast adenocarcinoma

Disease courses and treatment: right breast lump was found for three months which the needle biopsy showed breast cancer. On February 20 1995 she had the removal of the breast cancer and once radioactive therapy after the operation. Because of the weakness, she couldn't tolerate it. On May 11 1995 she started to take XZ-C1+XZ-C4 and continued to take them for more than three years. After she took the medicine, her energy level was improving and her appetite was increasing and her weight is increasing. Following up with us every month and her medical condition is stable.

Comments: this patient had the removal of the breast on Feb 20 1995 and once radioactive therapy after the operation. Because of the weakness the radiative therapy was stopped. In May 1995 she started to take the XZ-C1+XZ-C4. After three years her condition is stable. When she came back for her five year follow-up, she is healthy.

Case 11 Ms. Lee, female,33 year-old, Changda in Hunan, worker, Medical record number::3400667

Diagnosis: Left simple breast cancer.

Disease courses and treatment: On November 29 1996 she had the removal of the breast cancer in Changda which showed the right armpit lymph node metastasis(3/5). After one month, CMF was done which she used once/week, for more than four weeks.

On December 25 1996 she started to use XZ-C to protect her bone marrow. After taking the medicine, her whole blood went back to the normal level. From April 2 1997 to May 14 1997 she had radioactive 15 times in right breast inner line, 15 times under the armpit right and 25 times in the right breast outside lines. XZ-C were taken as the supplement therapy without the side effects. The patients is stable and reaction small and even no side effects when she took XZ-C with radiactherapy and chemotherapy. In June 2004 she only took XZ-C. Every three months she came to Wuhan to refill her medicines. Her condition is stable. In Dec 2004 when she came back to follow up with us, she is energetic and appetite is good and her face is glowing of the health. Acting is as the normal healthy persons. She came to refill her medicine from XXXX to WuHAN.

Comments: the curative experience of the treatment:1). During the radiacti and chemotherapy the XZ-C4 can reduce the reaction, during the interval time between the radiac and chemotherapy and after them XZ-C can strengthen longterm curative effects to protect the recurrency.2)after the surgery about six months the radia+chemotherapy +XZ-C can kill the remaining tumor cells or the small tumor lesions, meanwhile to protect the host immune organs. After taking the medicine for six months, the patient's general condition is good so that XZ-C can get rid of the wrong and strengthen the long-time curative effects. After 9 years of the operation, XZ-C can strengthen the long-term therapy.

Case 12 Ms Liu, female, 49 year-old, Changsha in Hunan, teacher, Medical record number::260003372

Diangosis: breast infiltrating ductal cancer.

Disease courses and treatment condition: in February 2005 a left breast lump was found which is 2cmx1.5cm, biopsy showed that high degree mutation. On March 8 2005 she had CAF. On May 30 2005 the breast cancer was removed partially, pathology showed the breast cancer so that the breast cancer radiact removal was performed Pathologyshowed that left breast cancer infiltrated ductal cancer. LN0/20 with the C-erB2(++), P53(+), PR(-),ER(-),nm23(+). After the surgery the chemotherapy was used for six cycles. On Octocber 22 2005 she started to take XZ-C to strengthen the curative effects and to prevent the recurrence and metastasis.

Comments:in this case before the operation the lymph nodes under armpit were palpatited. Chemotherapy for six cycle was used before the operation and after the operations to strengthen the long time curative effect. She persistently takes these medicine more than six years and her healthy condition is stable.

Case 13. Mr. Qian, male, 66year-old, Wuhan, accounting, Medical record number::5401066

Diangosis:rectal carcinoma

Disease courses and treatment conditions:occasionally diarria and constipation with bloody stool for two years. The rectal examination showed that there was a 3cmx3cm lump at the 6 clock point in the xxxx position. On January 20 1998 the colonoscopy showed the polypoid mutation of the rectal colon. On January 24 1998 Dixon which the 40cm of the colon were cut off was done in the xiehae hospital, Pathology showed that rectal cancer with middle division and invade into the muscular layer without lymph nodes metastasis and the margin clear. After thesurgcry, on March 3 1998 he started to use the XZ-C and took this medicine persistenly for more than eight years and he comc back to work for more than five years He is stable and still continued to use these medicine.

Comments: this case is rectal adenocarcinoma. In January 1998 Dixon was done and Pathology showed that rectal adenocarcinoma, middle-degree. After the operation he only took the XZ-C1+XZ-C4 for more tha eight years. His medical condition is stable.

Suggestions: After the rectal Dixon without the chemotherapy, he only took the immune regulation medicine XZ-C to protect his thymus and bone marrow to improve his immune functions to improve the life quality and prevent the recurrence and metasatasis. He was stable.

Case14 Ms Year-oldng, female, 32year-old, Zhaoyang, accounting, Medical record number::500993

Diagnosis: rectal villious adenocarcinoma

Disease courses and treatment condition: the patient had bleedy stool. In September 1997 the Colonoscopy and biopsy showed the rectal cancer. On September 17 1997 she had the rectal radial operation which showed that the lump was 1.0cmx1.0cm on the bases and was 4cm distance from the ana. Pathology reported the rectal villous adenocarcinoma and invaded into the all of the wall of the intestines with the menstema lymph node metastasis. After the operation she had chemotherapy once. Because of the decrease of the white blood cells she stop chemotherapy and started to use XZ-C1+XZ-C4. Her medical condition is well and stable. She continued to take the medicine for more than eight years only without chemotherapy and other therapy. She did her chores as the normal persons.

Comments:this case is the rectal radial removal on September 17 1997, during the operation, the metastasis were found in the mestaen membrane lymph nodes and invades the whole wall of the intestines. After the operation she had the chemotherapy once which had been stopped because the side effects were severe. Since December 3 1997 she started to take XZ-C only for more than eight years to prevent the reccurrence and metastasis after the surgery. Her medical condition is well.

Case 15 Mr. Yu, Male, 69year-old, Heilunjing, officer, Medical record number::6001181. Diangosis: the bladder transitional cell cancer

Diseases courses and treatment condition: The bloody urine on Februay 27 in 1998. On March 2 the cystoscopy and ultrasound showed that there was the round lump in the front wall, which is 1.6cmx1.4cm and growed toward to the cavity of the bladder and is the neoplasum of the front wall of the bladder. On March 10 in 1998 the surgery removed the tumor tissues in the bladder and Pathology showed that the bladder transitional cell tumors. He was told that this tumor is the recurrence of the tumors. After the surgery, he had once chemotherapy(on May 26 1998). His reaction to chemotherapy is severe such as the vomiting, nausea, and the whole body is uncomfortable. The left testicule enlarges so that he stop chemotherapy. On June 18 1998 he started to take the XZ-C. He follow up with us very month and his condition is good and his urine is normal and he doesn't have any other symptoms. He follow up with us for more than six years and he is healthy.

Comments: in this case on March 10 1998 the surgery removed three tumors in the bladder and Pathology showed that bladder transitional cell carcinoma. After the operation once chemotherapy was done which the patient had severe reaction to this chemotherapy. On June 18 1998 he started to take the medicine XZ-C1+XZ-C4+XZ-C6. He continued to take this medicine for more than seven years and his healthy condition is good without other therapy and without the recurrence and metasatasis.

Comments:

Case 16 Ms. Zhang, female,39 year-old, Wuhan, account, Medical record number::1700321

Diagnosis: the stomach cancer from the stomach ulcer, low differential adenocarcinoma

Disease courses and treatment: in March 1994 because of the uncomfortable in the upper abdomen for one month and getting worse for one week so that the endoscopy showed the stomach ulceration. On April 20 1994 the major stomach was removed and had chemotherapy for six courses of the treatment after the operation with xxxxx+xxxxx to protect the livers. Pathology showed the low differential stomach canciroma and had lymph nodes metastasis. On November

22 1995 he started to take XZ-C1+XZ-C4+XZ-C8 only to protect the bone marrow and follow up with us for more than ten years. He doesn't have metastasis and recurrence and his condition is great.

Comments: this patient had low degree adenocarcinoma in the stomach and lymph node metastasis. On April 20 1994 he had the removal of his major stomach, then he had six courses of the chemotherapy. On November 22 1995 he took the medicine only and followed up with us for more than ten years. His medical condition is great.

Suggustions: After the operation the combination of the chemotherapy and XZ-C medicine can improve the long-term treatment. XZ-C can prevent the cancer recurrence and metastasis.

Case 17 Mrs Hang, female, 65year-old, Huangpi in Hubei, Medical record number::10402074

Diagnosis: the middle esophogus carcinoma

Disease courses and treatment condition: In April 2001 the patient had difficulty swallowing and chest and back pain and gradually increased. Until June only can eat the liquid food and vomit the mucous staffs. On June 6 2001 the barium swallow tests in the xxx showed under the aorta branch xxxx 2cm there is a 10cm lenghth narrow and 6cm xxxxxlump in the left wall and the muscous stop. Because of the cost, she didn't have the operation, radioactive and chemotherapy. On June 25 she started to take XZ-C. After three months, her general condition is better and her appetite is getting better and the difficultying swallowing is getting better and can eat the rice soup, noodle. She continued taking the medicine until March 2002 then can take the rice and regular food. In July 2003 she just took XZ-C4+XZ-C2. In April 2005 when she followed up with us, she is energetic and her appetites was great at that time she had been taking XZ-C for more than five year. He condition is stable and can eat the regular food and can do light house work.

Comments: This patient had esophageal cancer which she only took XZ-C to control her condition without the operation, radiactiv therapy and chemotherapy. For more than four years, there was no metastasis and her condition had been controlled and can eat the regular food and rice. She is as healthy as other old persons and can do some choresevery day.

She kept taking her medicine regularly.

Case 18 Mr.Huang male, 66year-old, Huanpi, officer, Medical record number::300584

Diagnosis: the middle and low esophagous carcinoma

Disease courses and treatment:in March, he had the difficulty to swallow and the barium swallow test showed that the middle and low esophagum cancer. In May 1996 he had the removal of his cancer without other therapy. On June 19 1996 he started to use the XZ-C as the supplemental therapy to prevent the reccurrence and metastasis. He only takes XZ-C to protect his thymus and bone marrow for more than three years, then he changed into periodly taking the medicine. He is energetic and his appetite is good and walking and other activities are the same as the normal persons. In April 2005 when he came back to follow up with us, his condition is stable.

Comments: after the operation of his esophague, this patient only took XZ-C to assisting his therapymore than nine years, his condition is stable.

六. Chemotherapy plus Z-C Chinese medicine treatment of typical cases of acute lymphoblastic leukemia

Case Mr. Zhao, female, 34 year-old, Wuhan, officer, Medical record number:: 9801953
Diagnosis: Acute leukemia

Disease course and treatment: On Novermber 29 the patient was diagnosed as acute leukemia in Beijing hospital and was treated by chemotherapy for seven months. In August 2000 he was treated by bone morrow transplantation, however the results were not good after that because WBC, RBC and platelets are low. Such as wbc0.5x109/l, platelets were 5x100/l, HB46g/l. He depended on the blood transfusion, which were performed once per 8-9 days for 250ml. During his inpatient in Beijing, He had 10 times blood transfusion and 14 times platelets (once per 10 days).In Feb 2001 he came to Wuhan and on Feb 2, 2001 he started to use XZ-C1+XZ-C2+XZ-C8 to protect his thymus and his bone morrow. In April 2001 his WBC and RBC and Pletelets increase and stop to get transfusion. He takes XZ-C1+XZ-C2+XZ-C4 for more than one year and seven months and feel fine and he looked good and healthy and appetites increases and walking and runnig as the normal individual. In September 4 2003 he traveled to America and took his medicine XZ-C1+XZ-C2+XZ-C4 with him and he takes his medicine persistently.

In 2004 he immigrate into Canada and took his medicine XZ-C1+XZ-C2+XZ-C8 regularly and increase blood soups which will be filled once per 3 months. In April 2005 He called me and told us that he was healthy and his medical condition was controlled very well and appetite and sleep very well and started to work on business and energy level is perfectly well.

Comments: This patient has ALL and after seven months chemotherapy in August 2000, he had bono marrow transplantation. However the treatment results were not good because his blood counts were still low which he depended on the blood transfusion. On Feb 2 2001 he started to take XZ-C1+XZ-C2+XZ-C4. And increase blood soups etc. and after four months his blood counting went back the normal. After one year and seven months his blood counting keeps normal and he is healthy and has taken these medicine for more than 4 years and work in the business field and energy level is normal.

Suggustion: All can be treated satisfiedly by chemotherapy and XZ-C to protect the bone marrow and improve the immune system function. Now he has been followed up more than seven years and his healthy condition is very well.

16

The immune function of Chinese herbal medication in advanced cancer

1. Drugs that improve immune function should be used in the treatment of advanced cancer.

    1. Found from tumor research

        In the late stage of cancer, the mice have low immune function and progressive atrophy of the thymus.

        (1) In 1986, when we performed a tumor-bearing animal model experiment in our laboratory, we removed the thymus (THC) to produce a tumor-bearing animal model. Injection of immunosuppressants also contributed to the establishment of a tumor-bearing animal model. The conclusions of the study clearly demonstrate that there is a clear positive relationship between the occurrence and development of cancer and the immune function of the host and the tissue function of the immune organs. It is difficult to manufacture animal models without removing the thymus. Repeated experiments repeatedly confirmed the experimental results.

        (2) Whether it is low in immune function and then easy to get cancer, or cancer first, then immune function is low,

        Our experimental results are: first, there is low immunity and then easy to have cancer, if there is no immune function, it is not easy to vaccinate successfully.

        The results of this study suggest that: improving and maintaining good immune function, protecting immune organs Thymus (TH) is one of the important measures to prevent cancer.

        (3) Animal models for establishing liver metastasis when we study the relationship between metastasis and immunity in cancer

117

Divided into two groups, A and B. Group A used immunosuppressants, and group B did not.

RESULTS: The number of intrahepatic metastases in group A was significantly higher than that in group B.

The results of this experiment suggest that metastasis is associated with immunity, low immune function or the use of immunosuppressive agents, which may promote tumor metastasis.

(4) When our laboratory conducted an experiment to investigate the effects of tumors on the immune organs of the body, it was found that with the progress of cancer, TH was inhibited by progressive cell proliferation and its volume was significantly reduced.

The results of this experiment suggest that the tumor will inhibit TH, causing the immune organs to shrink or to be atrophy.

The above experimental results show that the occurrence, development and metastasis of cancer have a clear positive relationship with the decline of host immune function. The advanced cancer in mice has low immune function and progressive atrophy of Thymus. Therefore, in the treatment of advanced cancer, drugs that increase immune function should be used, and drugs that reduce or suppress immunity should not be used.

2. Experimental study on drugs for raising immunosuppressive tumors from natural Chinese herbal medicines

The above experimental results show that as the tumor progresses and the host's Thymus undergoes progressive atrophy, then can we use some methods to prevent the atrophy of the host Thyrnus?

(1) Animal models for establishing liver metastasis when we study the relationship between metastasis and immunity in cancer

Divided into two groups, A and B. Group A used immunosuppressants, and group B did not.

RESULTS: The number of intrahepatic metastases in group A was significantly higher than that in group B.

The results of this experiment suggest that metastasis is associated with immunity, low immune function or the use of immunosuppressive agents, which may promote tumor metastasis.

(2) When our laboratory conducted an experiment to investigate the effects of tumors on the immune organs of the body, it was found that with the progress of cancer, TH was inhibited by progressive cell proliferation and its volume was significantly reduced.

The results of this experiment suggest that the tumor will inhibit TH, causing the immune organs to shrink.

The above experimental results show that the occurrence, development and metastasis of cancer have a clear positive relationship with the decline of host immune function. The advanced cancer in mice has low immune function and progressive atrophy of Thymus. Therefore, in the treatment of advanced cancer, drugs that increase immune function should be used, and drugs that reduce or suppress immunity should not be used.

2. Experimental study on drugs for raising immunosuppressive tumors from natural Chinese herbal medicines

The above experimental results show that as the tumor progresses and the host's Thymus undergoes progressive atrophy, then can we use some methods to prevent the atrophy of the host Thymus?

To explore the atrophy of immune organs when stopping tumor progression, and to find ways to restore TH and restore immune function is to seek the drug of increasing immunity against cancer in natural medicines.

After long-term and batch-by-batch, 200 kinds of traditional Chinese herbal medicines that are considered to be "anti-cancer Chinese medicines" were tested for tumor suppression in tumor-bearing animals in our laboratory.

The results showed that 152 were ineffective, and only 48 of them had certain or even better inhibitory effects on cancer cell proliferation, and at the same time increased immunity. Among them, 26 Chinese herbal medicines (HM) have enhanced macrophage function or stimulated the weight of the thymus of the immune organ increases in the animals, or increase the white blood cells; or promote the proliferation of spleen lymphocytes, increase the lymphocyte transformation rate, enhance the immune function of T cells, enhance the activity of NK cells, promote the induction of interferon, optimize the combination, and then In vivo anti-tumor experiments in liver cancer, gastric cancer, S180 and other tumor-bearing animal models, further screening and eliminating the effects of non-stabilization, further screening and forming XZ-C immunoregulatory and anti-cancer traditional Chinese medicine, can protect Thymus and increase immune function, protect the marrow and produce blood, improve immune function.

Based on the successful screening of animal experiments, it has been applied in clinical practice. After 34 years of clinical verification of a large number of cases, XZ-C immunomodulation of traditional Chinese medicine can improve the quality of life of patients with advanced cancer, increase immunity, enhance physical fitness, and improve appetite, prolonged survival, the effect is more significant.

3. Experimental study on anti-tumor and immune enhancement of Fuzheng Peiben Chinese medicine on S_{180} mice

1. purpose

Through more than 40 years of research and practice on the prevention and treatment of malignant tumors by Chinese and Western medicine in China, it has been found that many traditional Chinese medicines have certain curative effects on the treatment of tumors; especially the research on the treatment of malignant tumors by Chinese medicine with Fuzheng Pei-Ping effect shows that Fuzheng Peiben Traditional Chinese medicine can enhance physical fitness, improve human immune function, improve quality of life and prolong survival. However, traditional Chinese medicine treatment of tumors is mostly observed in clinical experience, but no experimental research has been conducted. To explore whether the spleen, Yiqi Yangxue and Bushen Chinese medicine I Chinese medicine Fuzheng Peiden can inhibit tumor growth or not, therefore, the following experiment was carried out.

2. Method

(1) Experimental animals:

There were 160 Kunming mice, 5-6 weeks old, weighing 27 ± 2.0 g, half male and half female.

(2) Tumor-bearing animal model:

S180 ascites tumor cells were inoculated subcutaneously into the right forelimb axilla of each experimental rat according to $1 \times 10^7 \times 0.2$ mI tumor cell fluid.

(3) Experimental grouping.

The experimental animals were randomly divided into

Group A: Buzhong Yiqi treatment group (n=20):
Group B: qi and blood double supplement treatment group ((n-20);
Group C: nourishing kidney yin treatment group ((n-20);
Group D: Wenbu Shenyang treatment group ((n-20);
Group E: ATCA mixture treatment group ((n=20):

Group F: Xiaochaihu Tang treatment group ((n-20);

Group G: Compound capsule treatment group ((n-20);

Group H: tumor-bearing control group ((n-20).

The groups were started on the 2nd day after inoculation, and were administered with Chinese herbal medicines at 0. 4m1/(d·d) respectively. The tumor-bearing control group was treated with the same amount of normal saline.

(4) Preparation of traditional Chinese medicines in each group:

It is made into a modern dose of boiling and concentrated according to the original side, and the concentration of the crude drug is 200%. The above drug concentration and intragastric dose were obtained by replacing the normal human dose with the mouse dose.

In this experiment, the traditional Chinese medicines such as Buzhong Yiqi, Qixueshungbu, Nourishing Kidney Yin, Warming Kidney Yang, Attacking and Applying ATCA Mixture, Xiaochaihu Decoction and Compound Capsule were used to treat S180 mice.

(5) Observation project:

The tumor appearance time and tumor survival time of each group of mice were systematically observed, and their serum protein content, peripheral blood T lymphocyte count and weight of immune organs were measured.

3. The results

The combination of Fuzheng Peiben and Fuzheng Pei Ben as the main component of ATCA mixture can significantly delay the tumor emergence time and inhibit tumor growth (the inhibition rate of ABC, D, E group is 40%, 45%, 44. 5 %, 31% and 36%); The survival time of tumor-bearing mice was prolonged. (The survival periods of group A, B, C and D.E were 27.6%, 45%, 38.5%, 25%, 26.5%, respectively). Xiaochaihu Decoction, which is mainly based on cockroaches, could not significantly inhibit tumor growth and prolong survival (compared with group E, $P>0.05$).The serum protein content of group A, B, C, D..E increased, the A/G ratio increased, and the peripheral blood T lymphocyte count increased ($P<0.05$ compared with group G, P. O. 01), thymus atrophy is significantly inhibited.

4. In conclusion

This study demonstrates that Fuzheng Peiben or Fuzheng Peimoto is the main treatment of traditional Chinese medicine to inhibit tumor and enhance immunity. It can increase the level of peripheral blood T lymphocytes in different degrees, which is more effective than the treatment based on phlegm.

5. discuss

(1) Anti-tumor and prolonging survival of Fuzheng Peimoto Chinese medicine treatment.

Many cancer patients can clinically show "virtual" symptoms such as qi deficiency, blood deficiency, yin deficiency, and yang deficiency. The treatment should be treated with Fuzheng Peimoto Chinese medicine. This experiment explores the anti-tumor effect of Fuzheng Peiben's various methods and the combination of attack and compensation.

The results show:
Buzhong Yiqi, Qi and qi double supplement, nourishing kidney yin warming kidney yang, etc. Fuzheng Peiben traditional Chinese medicine and ATCA mixture based on Fuzheng Peiben traditional Chinese medicine treatment can significantly delay the occurrence of tumor inoculation in mice, inhibit tumor growth and prolong Tumor-bearing mice survive.
From the inhibition rate of each group:
In the qi and blood double-filled experimental group, the tumor inhibition rate reached 45%;
In the nourishing kidney yin experimental group, the tumor inhibition rate reached 44.5%.
Followed by Buzhong Yiqi, its anti-tumor effect is also 40%, and the effect is also good;
Again, the ATCA mixture has a tumor inhibition rate of 36%:
However, the effect of Wenbu Shenyang treatment group was poor, and the tumor inhibition rate was 31%.
It seems that in the inhibition of tumors, it is advisable to use the method of tonifying blood and nourishing kidney yin.
Analysis from the survival rate extension rate:
The qi and blood double supplement group reached 45%, which was the longest survival group;
The second is to nourish the kidney yin group, up to 38.5%, the effect is also good, as for the supplement of Zhongqi Yiqi, Wenbu Shenyang and the combination of the ATCA mixture treatment group, can also prolong the survival period, but less than the qi and blood double supplement and nourish Bushen Yin treatment group.
Xiaochaihu Decoction and Fufang Capsule treatment group, which were mainly based on phlegm and blood stasis, showed no significant inhibition of tumors in this group of experiments, and could not prolong the survival of tumor-bearing mice, and the effect was the worst.
Therefore, from the perspective of prolonging the survival period, the treatment of qi and blood double supplement and nourishing kidney yin is the first choice, followed by Buzhong Yiqi, Wenbu Shenyang and attack and supplement. From the two aspects of inhibiting tumor and prolonging survival, the best is qi and blood supplement, followed by nourishing kidney yin, followed by Buzhong Yiqi and ATCA mixture. The effect of warming kidney and kidney is not obvious.

As for the Xiaochaihu Tang and the compound capsules which are mainly based on cockroaches, no obvious effect is obtained from the results of this experiment.

In short, the treatments of Fuzheng Peiben and Fuzheng Peiben have different degrees of inhibition of tumor growth and prolonged survival, while the treatment based on phlegm-free has no obvious anti-tumor and prolong survival.

This experiment shows that:

The treatment of Fuzheng Peiben traditional Chinese medicine or Fuzheng Peiben traditional Chinese medicine is very obvious for the tumor inhibition of small volume tumors, and can significantly prolong the survival period and improve the quality of life.

Therefore, it is often used as one of the auxiliary treatments for postoperative radiotherapy and chemotherapy. Many literatures have reported that the use of Fuzheng Peiben in the treatment of malignant tumors has achieved good results. The results of this experiment further confirm that the treatment of qi and blood double supplement, nourishing kidney yin and Buzhong Yiqi can inhibit tumor and prolong survival. It provides an experimental basis for the clinical treatment of malignant tumors with integrated Chinese and Western medicine.

(2) The role of Fuzheng Peiben Chinese medicine treatment enhances body immunity

This experiment shows that the traditional Chinese medicine of Fuzheng Pei and the traditional Chinese medicine with Fuzheng Peiben can increase the level of peripheral blood T lymphocytes in different degrees. For example, at the 4th week, the T lymphocyte levels are: 41.5% of Buzhong Yiqi group.,

The qi and blood double supplement group was 44.8%, nourishing Shenyin group 38.6%, Wenbu Shenyang group 37. 5%. ATCA mixture group 35.6%; inhibiting thymus atrophy, such as the second week, Buzhong Yiqi, qi and blood double The thymus index of the tonic, nourishing kidney yin, warming kidney and aphrodisiac and AT CA mixture treatment group were significantly different from the tumor-bearing control group.

It is suggested that the anti-tumor effect of Fuzheng Peiben may be related to enhancing the immune function of the body.

Some people think that many plant polysaccharides have immunomodulatory properties, called anti-tumor polysaccharides. These polysaccharides cannot directly kill cancer cells, but they can activate the immune system in the body to release anti-tumor cytokines or enhance LAK cells. The killing effect on cancer cells.

Fuzheng Pei This medicine is rich in plant polysaccharides. For example, Zhao Kesheng reported that the polysaccharides from Huangmao were extracted and found to have a molecular weight of 20000-25 000. The peripheral blood mononuclear cells (PBMC) of normal human and tumor patients secrete tumor necrosis factor in vitro. (TNF) has a significant promoting effect.

Chen Kai and other reports:

Chinese herbal compound Fuzheng Kangliu liquid can promote the natural killer cell activity and interleukin-2 (IL-2) activity of transplanted S180 mice, and can promote the activation of

T lymphocytes, promote the phagocytosis of peritoneal macrophages, and increase the spleen. Thymus weight. In short, the role of Fuzheng Peiben in the human immune system is very complicated and needs further observation and research.

(3) Fuzheng Peiben traditional Chinese medicine treatment can enhance the body's ability to resist disease, enhance blood cells and enhance physical strength.

This experiment shows that:

Fuzheng Peizhi can increase the serum protein content of tumor-bearing mice and increase the ratio of clear/globulin. The clinical observation data of our oncology clinic showed that XZ-C, which is mainly based on Fuzheng Peiben, was applied to liver cancer, esophageal cancer, gastric cancer and colorectal cancer. Immune regulation inhibits cancer and promotes Chinese medicine. Both red blood cells and hemoglobin were higher than the control group, and leukopenia was also inhibited. It shows that Fuzheng Pei can enhance blood cells and proteins, enhance physical strength and improve disease resistance. Fuzheng Peiben has been widely used in clinical treatment as one of the treatments for the treatment of tumors with integrated Chinese and Western medicine. The results of this experiment show that: Fuzheng Peiji treatment can delay the tumor emergence time, inhibit tumor growth, prolong tumor-bearing survival, enhance the body's immune function and disease resistance, and improve the quality of life. It can provide experimental basis for clinical Chinese medicine to fight cancer.

4. The immune effect of Chinese herbal medicine on patients with advanced cancer

Patients with advanced cancer are mostly deficient, and common immune function is low.

Tonic and remedy medicine can enhance the body's immune function, which is of great significance for the prevention and treatment of tumor patients with low immune function.

1. Enhance non-specific immune function

(1) It can stimulate the thymus and spleen of animal immune organs to increase their weight:

For example, ginseng soup can increase the thymus weight of the young mice, which is 2.2 times that of the control group.

(2) Enhance the phagocytic function of macrophages:

Such as Angelica, and medlar (Wolfberry) can promote the phagocytic function of macrophages, especially the effect of qi medicine.

(3) Increase the number of peripheral white blood cells:

Such as Rehmannia, spatholobus, etc., can significantly increase the number of white blood cells.

2. Enhance cellular immunity

(1) Promote the proliferation of spleen lymphocytes: such as yam and mulberry parasitism can increase the proportion of T cells in peripheral blood.
(2) Increase the conversion rate of lymphocytes:

Such as white fungus and other tonic drugs, have the effect of increasing the rate of lymphocyte transformation.

(3) Enhance red blood cell immunity:

For example medlar (Wolfberry) can significantly increase the rosette rate of mouse erythrocyte C36 receptor (RBC-C36) and the erythrocyte-immunocomplex (RBC-IC) rosette formation rate.

3. Enhance humoral immunity

(1) Promote antibody production:

Such as meat from Rong, etc., have the effect of promoting antibody production, and the levels of serum IgG..IgAJgM and other antibodies are increased to varying degrees.

(2) Increase the number of spleen antibody-forming cells.

Injection of Epimedium polysaccharides can increase the production of spleen and cellular antibodies in mice by more than 1 time. The yam polysaccharide can significantly increase the number of spleen and hemolytic plaque forming cells in mice. However, some tonic drugs have a two-way effect of immune enhancement and inhibition.

5. The enhance function of the effect of Chinese herbal medication on immune function in tumor-bearing

In Chinese medicine, tumor formation and development are inadequate positive qi, and that positive qi deficiency associated with tumor occurrence, development, treatment and prognosis of the whole process. Righting training is a basic rule in the prevention and treatment of cancer medicine, and the most prominent is the body's immune function, particularly in the regulation of cellular immune function.

Modern studies have shown that occurrence, development and prognosis of tumor is closely related to cellular immune status in the cancer patients, the body immune function is suppressed and is in immunosuppression situation. This immune suppression is particularly evident in terminally ill patients or long after long treatment of chemotherapy or radiotherapy. Surgery, radiotherapy, chemotherapy can cause a decline in immune function. By Chinese medicine righting training to enhance immune function, thereby enhance the body cancer-fighting ability, improve the effectiveness of surgery, radiotherapy, chemotherapy, improve patient quality of life and prolong survival of patients.

1. The protection function of Chinese herbal medicines on immune organs

   In the experiments of protecting immune organs and increasing the weight of immune organs it was found:

   (1) Daily respectively fed mice with 15g / kg, 30g / kg extract Angelica and with 12.5mg / kg, 25mg / kg ferulic suspension for continuous 7d which could significantly increase mouse spleen and thymus weight.
   (2) Gavage mice with Polygonum 6g (kg • d) decoction, continuous 7d can significantly increase thymus weight and also antagonized prednisolone-induced immune organ weight decreases.
   (3) Littoralis polysaccharide 32mg / (kg • d), continuous 7 days can significantly increase thymus weight in mice by intraperitoneal injection.
   (4) Cistanche deserticola decoction can significantly increase the weight of spleen and thymus with fed mice.

   It must be noted that some herbs can reduce weight of immune organs and prompt immune organ atrophy, such as Hook, cicada, Puhuang, Sarcandrae, rhubarb, etc. Thymus atrophy, thymus cortical thinning, decreased cells and spleen weight was significantly reduced, splenic artery sheath surrounding the central lymphocytes (mostly T lymphocytes) decrease after fed 0.5g / d rhubarb decoction continuous 8d in normal mice. There is no significant effect on mice immune organs after perfusion medication 10mg / kg per day continuous 10d. Generally small dose had no effect, while large doses decreased.

2. The enhancement function of Chinese herbal medication on mononuclear phagocyte system

   Polysaccharide, Glycosides and a variety of other ingredients in Chinese herbal medications can enhance the mononuclear phagocyte system, particularly macrophage activity, enhance its immune function. Anti-tumor effect of macrophages are activated by tumor antigen through the T cells release specific macrophages, activated macrophages specifically kill tumor cells: macrophage-mediated cytotoxicity kill tumor cells, such as by activating the macrophages to secrete tumor necrosis factor (TNF), proteolytic enzymes, interferon (IFN) and others directly killing or inhibiting the growth of tumor cells.

(1) Medlar (Wolfberry) polysaccharides (LBP): Wang Ling etc. summarizes the research of immunomodulatory LBP effects in the second phase of "Shanghai Journal of Immunology"(1995): LBP with 0.125g / (kg • d) mice with 5d can enhance macrophage phagocytosis that LBP has a certain immune function. Zhang yongxiang and other like researched LBP effects on mouse peritoneal macrophages in tumor cell proliferation inhibition activity.

(2) Velvet polysaccharide (PAPS): can significantly improve macrophage function in immunocompromised induced by Hydrocortisone, namely with 0.01ug / ml concentration it has promotion function and has clear dose-effect relationship. PAPS has the strongest effect in 1ug / ml concentration.

(3) Gypenosides: Gypenosides with 300mg / (kg • d) once daily for continuous 7d can significantly enhance the ability of peritoneal macrophage cells in normal mice. In the "Wenzhou Medical College,"(1990) Volume 20(1) Shou Zhi Juan reported that macrophages volume increases and phagocytic digestion increases in lung and the abdominal loose connective tissue when mice were fed by Gypenosides with 50mg (containing 1.21% total glycosides) once daily for a month later.

(4) ABPS: can induce the synthesis of IL-1 and tumor necrosis factor (TNF-α) in macrophages. ABPS 25mg / kg or 50mg / kg can improve the LPS-induced IL-1 production by intraperitoneal injection. ABPS with 100mg / kg can promote the formation of TNF-α by intraperitoneal injection and it has the same strength role as BCG.

(5) Psoralen: with carcinogens Urethane cause lung cancer in mice, then intraperitoneally injection of psoralen 1mg / 20g the body weight, continuous 10d can significantly enhance lung cancer mouse peritoneal macrophage phagocytosis.

3. Chinese medication with enhancing the role of T cells immune function

T cells are very important in body's immune cells, not only will lead to specific cellular immune, and is involved in immune regulation, and other functions. Tumor cells are often accompanied by changes in cell surface antigens. Because of immune surveillance of T cells, T cells sensitized by tumor antigen can directly kill tumor cells or and release cytokines to kill T cell by directly or indirectly cytotoxicity.

(1) Epimedium polysaccharide (EPS): EPS with 100mg / Kg/ d for continuous 5d significantly increased peripheral WBC and T lymph cells by subcutaneous injection.

(2) Alfalfa Polysaccharides (MPS): in vitro can enhance lymphocyte proliferation induced by PHA, CONA, LPS and pokeweed (PWM). MPS 125mg / (kg · d) and 250 mg / (kg · d) significantly increased spleen lymphocyte index and the number of lymphocytes

by intraperitoneal injection. MPS also partially antagonized lymphocytes decrease induced by cyclophosphamide in intraperitoneal injection.

(3) Medlar polysaccharide (Wolfberry) (LBP): can significantly increase the percentage of peripheral external T lymphocytes in mouse. LBP 5mg / (kgxd) increases peripheral blood lymphocyte count by abdominal injection for continuous 7d. The control group was 65.4%, 81.6% for the treatment group, but increasing the dose does not continue to improve this effect. In T lymphocyte mitogen CONA inducing conditions, a small dose of LBP (5-10mg / kg) can also cause lymphocyte proliferation which means LBP can significantly promote T cell proliferation.

(4) Moutan: 12. 5 / kg and 25g / kg doses orally can significantly improve the mice's T lymph cell transformation. Radix paeonail rubra(TPG): 25g / kg dose orally can significantly improve mice IL-2 activity. Wulingzhi: dose 12.5g / kg and 25 g / kg not only can significantly improve the T lymphocyte function in mice, but also 25g / kg dose also significantly increased IL-2 activity in mice by Gavage.

It must be noted, herbs also have to inhibit T cell immune function, such as Sophora, turmeric, Hook, Millettia, rhubarb, etc. which reduction of T cell immune function must be caution.

4. The role of traditional Chinese medication on LAK cells

(1) Wind polysaccharide in a certain concentration range can be significantly increased IL-2-induced LAK cell killing activity.

(2) The sea buckthorn increases blood circulation. In tumor-bearing mice sea buckthorn juice (3g / kg) can significantly improve their spleen NK cells and LAK activity by injected intraperitoneally.

(3) Cao wenguang etc. found that three kinds of traditional Chinese medications such as APS, PAS and LBP could significantly promote the proliferation of mouse spleen cells with 5- 30mg / kg intraperitoneal injection in C57BL / 6 mice and. The spleen cells were $2X10^6$ / ml with 125-1,000U / ml of rlL-2 induced 4d, APS group found that injections of spleen cells LAK activity of the group increased by 70%) - 120% compared with normal saline; injection PAS group increased by 20 % -90%; injection LBP group by 26% -80%.

(4) Cao wenguang etc treated 79 cases of advanced cancer patients which didn't have good response to radiotherapy and chemotherapy with traditional Chinese medicine LBP combined with LAK, IL-2 from February 1992 to November 1993. LBP with oral dose 1. 7mg / kg, LAK total doses 1.2-32X 10^{10}, IL-2 with 3. 4- 4. 8X10^{7}U / person, specific programs in the conventional therapy is stopped after a month, give LBP 3 weeks after injection riL-2, giving LBP 4 week After a large number of patients with autologous PBL isolated LAK cells in vitro, reinfusion after various inspection, and then continue to give LBP and work L-2, 1 weeks. Results : 75 cases of evaluable patients, LAK / IL-2 combined with the efficacy of LBP group (36.36%) than single

with LAK / IL-2 effect group (18%), the former combined LBP group before and after treatment and NK activity of PBL 500U / ml IL-2 induced the LAK activity increased level significantly higher than the latter alone LAK / IL-2 group. Show LBP could significantly promote NK and LAK cells antitumor activity.

The regimens of strength spleen, warm yang, supporting kidney, YiQi, Yangyin etc increase LAK activity in vivo.

5. Immune function regulation of traditional Chinese medication on red blood cell (RBC)

In 1981 according to adhesion phenomena of RBC and the facts of type I complement variant (CR1) combining with immune complexes (IC) on the surface of RBC American scholar Siegel and others put forward to the concept of "red cell immune function", illustrated not only the respiratory function of red blood cells, and is involved in a variety of immune and immune regulate in the body: such as the removal of circulating immune complexes, and promote phagocytosis, immune regulation of lymphocyte. The red blood cells is involved in the production of IFN-7, IL2 antibodies and the regulation of natural killer cells (NK cells), lymphokine-activated killer cells (LAK cells) and phagocytic immune cells and so on.

(1) It was found that Astragalus (Astragalus polysaccharide, APS) enhances the activity of erythrocyte C3bR attached to the tumor cells and immune function in cancer patients in vitro. APS enhances erythrocyte immune function in cancer patients.

(2) In the group of Trichosanthes root(TCS) treatment and of untreated group in Ehrlich ascites carcinoma in mice it was found that in the untreated group RBD-C_3bR rosette rate was significantly lower than the normal group, the treatment group RBC-C_3bR rosette rate significantly higher than the untreated group and slightly higher than the normal group, which means mice RBC-C3bR activity was significantly decreased in the cancer mice and Trichobitacin can increase RBC-C_3bR activity significantly.

TCS influence on mice erythrocyte SOD activity: After the mice inoculated with cancer cells to 11d, the treatment group erythrocyte SOD activity was significantly higher than the untreated group and the normal group. Late tumor-bearing mice decreased erythrocyte SOD, this experiment shows Chinese medication TCS can restore and enhance the activity of SOD.

TCS influence on the ability of immune adhesion of red cell to tumor cells: with Ehrlich ascites tumor cells as target cells, to determine the TCS effect on the capability of the adhesion of immune in mice red blood cell to breast tumor cell, it was found 11 day after tumor cell inoculation tumor erythrocyte rosette rate(11.90±5.00)% in non-treatment mice was significantly lower than the normal mice (22.13 ±6.28)%; while in treated mice tumors erythrocyte rosette rate(26. 54± 7.27)% was slightly higher than the normal group was significantly higher than the untreated group.

TCS's effect on erythrocyte immune function in cancer patients: it have also a significant enhancement of the adhesion ability of the red blood cells to tumor cells in cancer patients. Tests found that cancer patients directly enhance rosette rate of RBC-C_3bR effect which there is a significant difference with normal saline (NS) group, and this role of the promotion has dose-dependent manner.

6. Types of biological medicine and its component response regulator (BRMS) action

Chinese medicine has a very important characteristic which has the role of two-way adjustment for biological therapy which can restore the body immune function to the normal direction.

In 1983 Jingjianping found that Astragalus can significantly increase IL-2 in "spleen false" mice model, but have no effect on normal mice.

In 1991 Xungxiaolin etc studied the effects of Millettia, FruitofPurpleflowerHolly, Psoralen Chinese medication on IL-2 production in mouse spleen cells and found that these drugs in three groups such as immunocompromised, hyperthyroidism, normal showed increased, inhibition, no influence which reflect double-acting medicine. Besides traditional Chinese medicine on the body due to the impact of anti-tumor substance and the amount thereof are closely related. Medlar at low concentrations can promote IL 3-secretion, but high concentrations inhibit IL-3 levels. When total glucosides of peony increase IL-2 production in the low concentrations by a dose-dependent. After the concentration exceed 12. 5mg, it will inhibit IL 2-secretion.

Chinese medication has been used in our country for thousands of years and many Chinese medications can have the roles of BRMS which the research of anti-cancer immune agents will have a bright future. Chinese medication by oral has mild adverse reactions. Compared with genetic engineering BRMS and exogenous IL-2, IFN TNF, the advantages of traditional Chinese medication similar to BRMS has the whole body anticancer role in the body immune system and can be repeatedly administered with non-toxic side effects, and is available for tumor, chemotherapy, radiotherapy-induced immune dysfunction, boost the immune cell activation so that endogenous cytokines can be released and cause inhibition of tumor growth.

In modern cancer treatment, Chinese medication can at least play a role in three areas: ① enhance the role of inherent anti-cancer member effect in the body, enhance the body's anti-cancer cell system (NK cells, TK cells, LAK cell factor); ② Some traditional Chinese medicine has a direct anti-cancer effect; ③ some medicine ingredients can reduce side effects of radiation therapy, chemotherapy, and reduce the inhibition to the white cells and help to recover, even increase radiotherapy and chemotherapy anti-cancer effect.

The background and experience of research topics

1. The source background of the project and the completion of the project (tortured)

My three monographs are actually the key scientific and technological projects undertaken by the "Eighth Five-Year Plan" during the "Eighth Five-Year Plan" period. "Project Name: "Experimental and clinical studies of furtherly discovering the anti-metastasis and anti-metastatic Chinese herbal medicine for the prevention and treatment of liver cancer, gastric cancer and precancerous lesions. The special title of the "Eighth Five-Year" National Science and Technology Research Project Special Contract: "Clinical and Experimental Research on the Treatment of Gastric Cancer and Precancerous Lesions by Chinese and Western Medicine" is headed by the National Science and Technology Commission.

In April 1991, the author submitted an application to the State Science and Technology Commission for key scientific and technological projects during the "Eighth Five-Year Plan" period. The project name is "Experimental and clinical research on the combination of Chinese and Western prevention and treatment with exploring anticancer and anticancer Chinese herbal medicine for the precancerous lesions of gastric cancer, liver cancer and gastric cancer."

Director Tian of the Hubei Provincial Science and Technology Commission in June organized the three project leaders of the province to apply for the National Science and Technology Commission project (1 person from Tongji Medical College, 1 from Hubei Medical College, 1 from Hubei College of Traditional Chinese Medicine) went to Beijing to report to the Chinese Medicine Administration of the Ministry of Health.

Two months later, Director Tian of the Provincial Science and Technology Commission and three project leaders went to Beijing to report further to the Ministry of Health on design and acceptance of the project. Two months later, when the project task was released and the "Eighth Five-Year National Science and Technology Research Project Contract" was being signed, Professor Xu Ze suddenly developed acute myocardial infarction, anterior wall and high wall myocardial infarction. After rescue and treatment, he was hospitalized for half a year, and he was relieved after a half-year break after leaving the hospital. The National Science and Technology Commission will also be stranded and suspended.

In 1993, Professor Xu Ze's physical health gradually recovered, and he also thought about continuing to study the content of the subject. Because the author has followed up the patients after high-cost radical resection, the results showed that postoperative recurrence and metastasis of cancer are the key factors affecting the long-term outcome after radical resection. It is necessary to study the clinical basis and effective methods to prevent postoperative recurrence and metastasis. Dr.Xu determined to do some research work that he could do and do what he can, but he had no idea but no research funding, so he started to find ways to raise funds for my own research. In 1993, when the author was retired, she applied for a clinic, and her meager income started as a research fund. Kunming mice were purchased from the Animal Center of the Medical College for animal experiments, and various animal cages and related equipment and instruments for experiments were started. Animal experiments were started. The meager income of the clinic is used to support Professor Xu Ze's animal experiments and scientific research, and to save money in careful calculation. The 6 rooms on the second floor are used for animal experiments.

In 1996, Professor Xu Ze was 63 years old and applied for retirement. After that, with the support of this meager income, a series of experimental research and clinical verification work were carried out. After 16 years of hard work and hard work, we finally completed the research project of the State Science and Technology Commission. We collected experimental and clinical research materials, data and summaries, and published three monographs:

1. "New understanding and new model of cancer treatment", Xu Ze, published by Hubei Science and Technology Press, January 2001, Xinhua Bookstore issued;
2. "New Concepts and New Methods for Cancer Transfer Treatment", Xu Ze, published by People's Military Medical Press, January 2006, issued by Xinhua Bookstore nationwide. In April 2007, the General Administration of Press of the People's Republic of China issued the "Three One Hundred" original book certificate.
3. "New Concepts and New Methods of Cancer Treatment" by Xu Ze and Xu Jie was published by Beijing Military Medical Press in October 2011. Later, the American medical doctor Dr. Bin Wu and others translated into English. The English version was published in Washington, DC on March 26, 2013, and is distributed internationally.

2. Some experiences

In the past, the author carried out scientific research work in medical colleges, with the guidance of superiors and colleagues, and the laboratory conditions were excellent. He had undertaken the National Natural Science Foundation, the National Science and Technology Commission, and the Provincial Science and Technology Commission. He has achieved two scientific research results. The project is at the domestic advanced level, one is the international advanced level, and won the second prize of Hubei Province Science and Technology Achievements twice, and won the first prize of Hubei Provincial Health Science and Technology Achievements.

But now it is different. Under such special circumstances, in a clinic or clinic, under the condition of unconditional and no equipment, how can we carry out and complete the national task?

The author has the following brief experience.

1. Self-reliance and self-raising. See the outpatient service for the patient service, and the outpatient income is used as research funding.
2. Keep outpatient medical records and follow up throughout the process.
3. Establish special scientific research collaborations, collaborate and cooperate according to scientific research plans.
4. Establish detailed medical records (including epidemiological data of patients), and analyze in depth the success of each treatment, the failure lessons and the particularity of the condition.
5. Adopting scientific research cooperation strategy of instrument sharing, equipment sharing and results sharing, we do not add large-scale instruments and equipment, but cooperate with the medical college affiliated school, and the high-precision equipment inspections are carried out in the medical college affiliated hospital.
6. Selecting scientific frontier topics, failing to declare the subject (because it has been nearly ancient and rare), and to study the results, only to the Ministry, the province, the city, and the scientific research results.
7. In the private outpatient department, the old professors can also carry out the research and cooperation with universities and colleges, the sharing of instruments and equipment, and the strategy of sharing results, making full use of the advanced equipment conditions of colleges and universities and combining their decades of clinical experience. Complete research projects.

After 20 years of hard work and hard work, we carried out a series of experimental research and clinical verification work, and finally basically completed the "Eighth Five-Year" research project of the National Science and Technology Commission that I applied for, and will study experimental and clinical research data, data, and conclusions. He has compiled more than 100 research papers. Because there is no research funding, he can't publish magazines according to papers. He is published according to new books, and has published two monographs.

Now published is the third monograph, "New Concepts and New Methods for Cancer Therapy."

These three monographs are three difficult stages of our hard-hitting, difficult climb, one step at a scientific research footprint, three different levels of results, three different peaks, which are a series of coherent scientific research steps and scientific research processes.

The above briefly describes the background and ins and outs of my three monographs:

From the results of a clinical follow-up to the discovery of experimental tumor research;

From the review of the clinical case of a medical practice to the analysis of adjuvant chemotherapy cases, evaluation, reflection, found that the drawbacks of traditional chemotherapy. Looking for anti-cancer and anti-metastatic new drugs from natural medicines (Chinese medicines), in vitro and in vivo experiments on cancer-bearing models, and found that XZ-C series of immunoregulatory Chinese medicines have been repeatedly tested in clinical trials. Now there are 16 years and 1 2000. Many cases were clinically validated.

From the experimental basic research and clinical verification observation to the theoretical understanding, a series of innovative theories are proposed, some are original innovations, and a series of reform measures for traditional therapies are proposed, and the strategies and strategic prospects for conquering cancer are proposed. Some of the above research contents and scientific research results are some of the original innovative intellectual property research papers that were first reported internationally. They are each populated in three of my monographs and published in the form of books.

ZC (XUZE China) immune regulation of anti-cancer, anti-metastatic series of traditional Chinese medicine preparations after 7 years of animal experiments, many years of oncology clinic outpatients a large number of advanced cancer clinical patients verified, the vast majority of patients can improve symptoms, relieve pain, more people with metastasis It can stabilize or control the disease, improve the quality of life, and prolong the survival period. It has a significant effect.

However, it has not been promoted.

A large number of patients with advanced cancer in the province and the country cannot benefit from it.

Many patients with cancer metastasis urgently need anti-metastatic and relapsed XZ-C immunomodulatory drugs, so they should try to promote the transformation of scientific research results.

XZ-C immunoregulatory series of drugs Our laboratory has long-term research and screening of long-term cancer-bearing animals and long-term clinical application verification to observe the self-developed traditional Chinese medicine preparations, all of which are original intellectual property rights of independent innovation or independent innovation. It is still:

1. "Is not known in the deep public"
2. How can I get out of the "squat"?
3. three major reasons to lock " Yuzhong",

    1. There are more than 10 items in the XZ-C1-10:

        Which one to develop? There are 7-8 auxiliary treatments such as water-removing soup and yellowing soup. Which one to develop?

2. Development of one, need 3 to 5 million yuan, no development funds.
3. There is no investment in the development of pharmaceutical companies that pass GMP.

We attach great importance to the construction of independent intellectual property rights, adhere to the research results of our own independent innovation in pharmaceuticals and formulas, and now have 16 kinds of XZ-C immunomodulatory anti-cancer and anti-metastatic series of independent intellectual property rights. The screening of cancer animal experiments and the clinically validated scientific research protocol preparations for a large number of patients with advanced cancer in the long-term have presented varying degrees of innovation and innovation. They are well received by the majority of patients and hope to get out of the anti-metastasis road with Chinese characteristics.

3. The social benefit assessment:

Cancer is the common disease of human ribs in human life, accounting for the first and second causes of death among urban residents in China. It is self-evident that cancer is still one of the medical problems. At the beginning of the 21st century, the most important problem in cancer treatment is metastasis. The most urgent problem to be solved now is how to resist metastasis, but the transfer is only a phenomenon, an understanding, and a target. Invisible, intangible, how to be specific, how to clearly understand the specific process, steps and mechanism of cancer metastasis, we propose anti-cancer metastasis as the target of the goal, in order to achieve this goal, the goal of anti-metastasis, measures must be specific, otherwise In this book, 14 new discoveries, new theories, and new concepts are proposed to address the process of cancer cell metastasis. For example, in this book, what is the current cancer research? The Key is anti-transfer or to anti-metastasis.

It has been discovered and proposed that cancer is manifested in three forms in human body. This third form is cancer cells on the way to metastasis: this new understanding, the new doctrine initiative will cause a series of changes and updates in the chain reaction. The goal of discovering and proposing cancer treatment should be directed to these three forms; Discovered and made two first-line on the whole process of the development of cancer, cancer treatment should be considered not only pay attention to two points, more attention should be paid off line; Specific measures should be found to transfer resistance transfer is the way cancer cells Weizhui interdiction; Find and treat cancer initiative new concepts, new models of immune therapy should be carried out eleven new models; Discover and propose a new model of cancer metastasis treatment, and propose a "three-step" for anti-cancer metastasis treatment. Some of the above new understandings, new theoretical insights, new concepts, important academic significance and important academic value, Discover and propose a new model of cancer metastasis treatment, and propose a "three-step" of anti-cancer metastasis treatment. Some of the above new understandings, new theoretical insights, new concepts, important academic significance and important academic value, which will have an important impact on the development of oncology medical science, and it may benefit the patients with millions of cancer metastasis, and come out with a new path to overcome cancer. How to find measures to prevent cancer cell metastasis, and how to explore it? In the research of anti-cancer, Chinese medicine is China's advantage, develop the role of this advantage in anti-metastasis research, give play to China's advantages, and catch up with the international advanced level. In this book, XZ-C immunomodulation anti-cancer anti-metastatic Chinese medicine, after 3 years of experimental screening of tumor-inhibiting rate in cancer-bearing animal models, and 11 years of clinical verification application, not only for the benefit of millions of cancer metastasis patients, but also The country has gained billions of economic benefits.

The experimental research pictures

1. Thymus atrophy of cancer-bearing Mouse

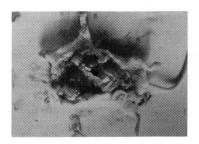 

Experimental surgery play a very important role in developing the medical secience and it is one key to open up the out-of-bounds area of the medical science. The preventive and curing ways of many diseases are applied to the clinic and promote the development of the medical science only when the stable achievements have been made through the experimental research on animal for many times

2. Animal Model for Experimental Research on Anti-cancer Metastasis and Recurrence

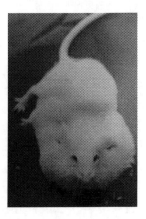

Cancer-bearing animal model with the cancerous block is exfoliative as a whole

136

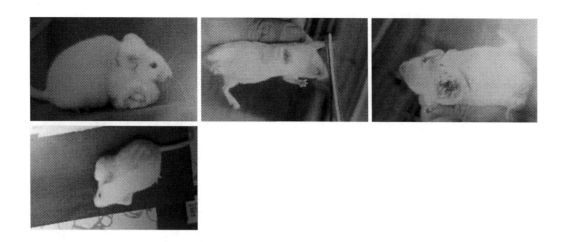

3. Treatment with ATCA in tumor-bearing group with S180 Sarcoma

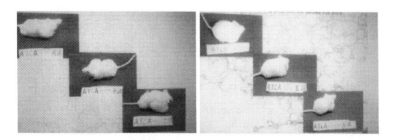

4. **The Experimental Research on Protecting Thymus and Increasing Immune Function as well as Protecting Bone Marrow and Hematopoiesis by XZ-C Medications**

    A. Treatment Group with XZ-C1 Medication and Control group using Cyclophosphamide(CTX)

        20 days after inoculation of Liver cancer H22
        XZ-C1 Treatment group   Control group

20 days after inoculation of Liver cancer H22

| Tumor | Thymus | Spleen | Kidney | Liver |

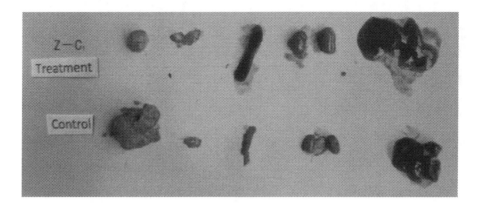

B. Treatment Group with XZ-C4 Medication and Control group using CTX

20 days after inoculation of Liver cancer H22

XZ-C1 Treatment group   Control group

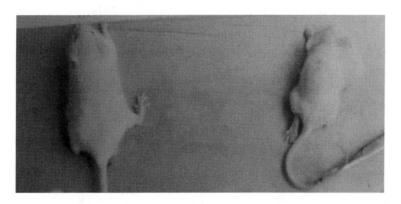

20 days after inoculation of Liver cancer H22

| Tumor | Thymus | Spleen | Kidney | Liver |

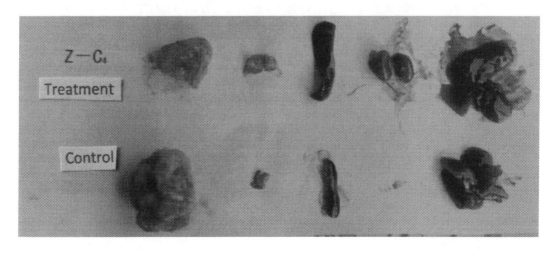

C. XZ-C5 Treatment group and Control group using CTZ

15 days after inoculation of Liver cancer H22
XZ-C5 Treatment   Control

15 days after inoculation of Liver cancer H22
Tumor   Thymus   Spleen   Kindey   Liver

Printed in the United States
By Bookmasters